ILLUSTRATED ATLAS OF THE WORLD

Alexander Gordon Smith

Published by Armadillo Books
an imprint of
Bookmart Limited
Registered Number 2372865
Trading as Bookmart Limited
Desford Road
Enderby
Leicester
LE19 4AD

ISBN 1-90046-584-1
Reprinted 2002, 2003

Produced for Bookmart Limited by
Nicola Baxter
PO Box 215
Framingham Earl
Norwich Norfolk
NR14 7UR

Designers: Amanda Hawkes and Sarah Crouch
Production designer: Amy Barton
Editors: Nicola Baxter and Jenny Knight
Cartographic editor: Sue Backhouse

Maps: Mountain High Maps® Copyright © 1993 Digital Wisdom, Inc.
Illustrations: Peter Bull Art Studio
Photographs: Corel Professional Photos throughout
except p32 top: Bengt Lundberg/Still Pictures
p32 centre: Martin Specht/Still Pictures
p32 bottom: Mark Edwards/Still Pictures

Printed in Singapore

Contents

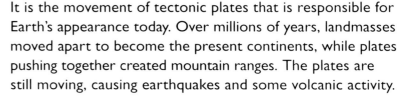

The World

Our Earth is one of nine planets that orbit the giant star we call the Sun. It has a solid inner core of iron and nickel, and a liquid metal outer core. Surrounding the core is a thick layer of rock, called the mantle. This makes up most of the Earth's mass. The exterior of the planet is formed from a thin layer of solid rock, like the skin of an apple, called the crust.

The Earth's crust and the upper mantle—together called the lithosphere—are not in one piece but formed from several large chunks of rock. These slabs are called tectonic plates. They can be many thousands of kilometres long but often less than 20 kilometres (12 miles) thick. There are seven main pieces of the lithosphere and many smaller ones.

It is the movement of tectonic plates that is responsible for Earth's appearance today. Over millions of years, landmasses moved apart to become the present continents, while plates pushing together created mountain ranges. The plates are still moving, causing earthquakes and some volcanic activity.

Earth is home to a huge variety of terrains and climates. Some of the main ones are shown in the photographs below.

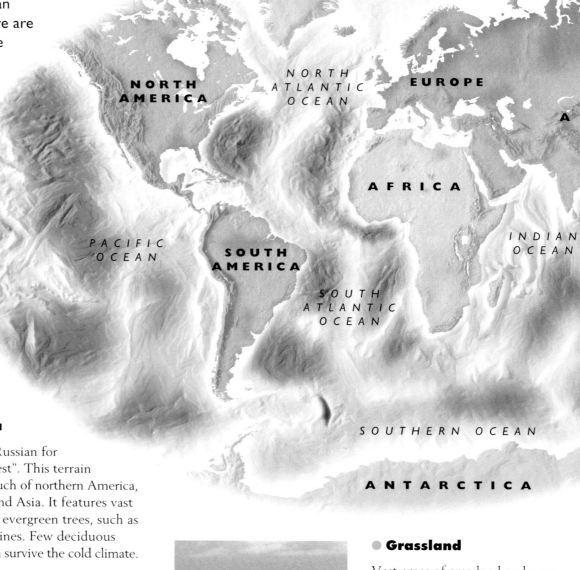

● Rainforest

Near the equator, abundant rain and high temperatures enable giant rainforests to thrive in South America, Asia and Africa. Millions of species of insects, birds, animals and plants flourish in this ideal habitat.

● Taiga

Taiga is Russian for "cold forest". This terrain covers much of northern America, Europe and Asia. It features vast forests of evergreen trees, such as firs and pines. Few deciduous plants can survive the cold climate.

● Temperate

A temperate region is one that is neither very hot nor very cold. The northern areas of Europe and America are temperate zones, once covered by vast forests. Over the centuries, large areas have been cleared for farming.

● Grassland

Vast areas of grassland make up the centres of several continents. Dry grassland areas, such as the North American prairies and the Russian steppes, have cold winters but warm summers. Tropical grassland is often found between equatorial rainforests and deserts. The savannah grasslands of central Africa are hot with periodic rain.

Mapping the World

A map shows features of the Earth's surface as they appear viewed from above. However, because the Earth is round, only a globe can show such features in a true relationship to each other. Of course, globes cannot be used in books, so mapmakers use a technique called projection to show a curved landscape on a flat surface.

The problem with projecting a sphere onto a flat map is that it is impossible to show both areas and distances accurately. In order to "flatten" the Earth's surface, it has to be divided into segments, like peeling the skin from an orange. This leaves large gaps that make the map difficult to use.

To produce a world map without gaps, certain areas have to be stretched. Several different types of map projection are employed, depending on what the map will be used for, but they all involve distorting parts of the world. On the globe below, for example, Antarctica appears as a landmass in its correct size and shape. On the projection next to it, the landmass has been stretched out.

I A

PACIFIC
OCEAN

OCEANIA

● Mountainous

Hot days, cold nights and strong winds mean that few plants and animals can be found in mountainous regions. Soil is scarce on steep slopes as it is easily washed away by rain. Above a certain altitude, called the tree line, trees cannot grow. The tops of mountains are often permanently covered in snow.

● Polar and tundra

The frozen Polar Regions lie around the North and South Poles. Thick ice covers much of this area all year round. To the south of the North Pole lies the tundra, a very cold and dry area, where the ground is permanently frozen.

● Longitude and latitude

Many maps show lines of latitude and longitude. These imaginary lines circle the globe from east to west (latitude) and from Pole to Pole (longitude). The line of latitude along which the Earth's circumference is greatest is called the equator, and lines of latitude are measured in degrees north and south of this line. Lines of longitude are measured in degrees east and west of the prime meridian, which runs through Greenwich in London, England, and represents 0° longitude.

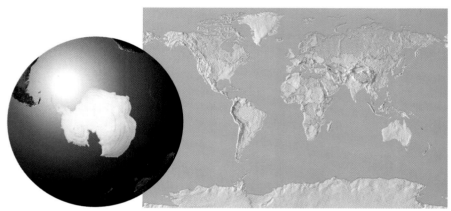

line of longitude

line of latitude

equator

prime meridian

The Earth spins on an imaginary axis that passes through the Poles.

● Desert

Large areas of Australia, Africa, the Americas and Asia are made up of dry, sandy or rocky desert. Temperatures can reach over 40°C (104°F) in the shade. Small areas of vegetation (oases) occur where an underground stream comes to the surface.

● Mediterranean

This kind of climate is named after the region surrounding the Mediterranean Sea between Europe and Africa. Summers are hot and dry, but winters are cooler and wetter. Plants such as orange and olive trees thrive in these conditions.

THE AMERICAS

N W E S

ARCTIC OCEAN

CHUKCHI SEA

BEAUFORT SEA

Baffin Bay

BERING SEA

ALASKA

Yukon   Porcupine

▲ Mt. McKinley

ALASKA RANGE

Mackenzie

ALEUTIAN ISLANDS

Gulf of Alaska

▲ Mt. Logan

LABRADOR SEA

MACKENZIE MOUNTAINS

Peace

Hudson Bay

C A N A D A

LAURENTIAN PLATEAU

Athabasca

G R E A T

Saskatchewan

Mt. Rainier ▲

Missouri

GREAT LAKES

ROCKY

CASCADE RANGE

Platte

P L A I N S

Mississippi

Missouri

APPALACHIAN MOUNTAINS

Cape Cod

SIERRA NEVADA

M O U N T A I N S

GREAT BASIN

Arkansas

Mt. Whitney ▲

Grand Canyon

Colorado

UNITED STATES OF AMERICA

Red

Mississippi

Alabama

Moving islands

Hawaii, over 3,200 kilometres (2,000 miles) west of the Americas, consists of a chain of 132 islands formed from the lava that a moving tectonic plate allows to break through the Earth's crust.

MEXICO

WESTERN SIERRA MADRE

EASTERN SIERRA MADRE

MEXICAN PLATEAU

Rio Grande

SARGASSO SEA

GULF OF MEXICO

Santiago

▲ Mt. Citlaltépetl

Balsas

GREATER ANTILLES

CARIBBEAN SEA

BELIZE

HONDURAS

GUATEMALA

EL SALVADOR   **NICARAGUA**

COSTA RICA

This great landmass comprises two distinct continents, joined by a narrow strip of land called the Isthmus of Panama and surrounded by the Atlantic and Pacific Oceans.

The Americas encompass an incredible variety of landscapes, from the icy wastelands of northern Canada to the blue seas and white sands of the Caribbean. Movement in the Earth's crust has created vast mountain ranges that dominate the west coasts of both continents—the Rockies in the north and the Andes in the south.

The Amazon River stretches for over 6,500 kilometres (4,000 miles) through South America. It is the world's second longest river. In contrast, the Atacama Desert, which lies in northern Chile, is one of the driest places in the world. Its parched, dusty landscape is unable to support any kind of life.

Rare habitats

The state of Florida, USA, is home to the Everglades. This is a unique ecosystem with an amazing range of wildlife. It is the only place in the world where alligators and crocodiles live side by side.

Named after Amerigo Vespucci, one of the first Europeans to sail across the Atlantic Ocean, the Americas form an enormous landmass stretching from the Arctic Circle to Cape Horn.

fact chart

NORTH AMERICA
- Area: 25,349,000 sq km (9,787,249 sq mi)
- Largest lake: Lake Superior, 83,270 sq km (32,150 sq mi)
- Longest river: Mississippi–Missouri, 6,019 km (3,740 mi)
- Highest mountain: Mt McKinley, 6,194 m (20,320 ft)

SOUTH AMERICA
- Area: 17,835,000 sq km (6,886,094 sq mi)
- Largest lake: Lake Titicaca, 8,340 sq km (3,220 sq mi)
- Longest river: Amazon, 6,570 km (4,080 mi)
- Highest mountain: Aconcagua, 6,960 m (22,834 ft)

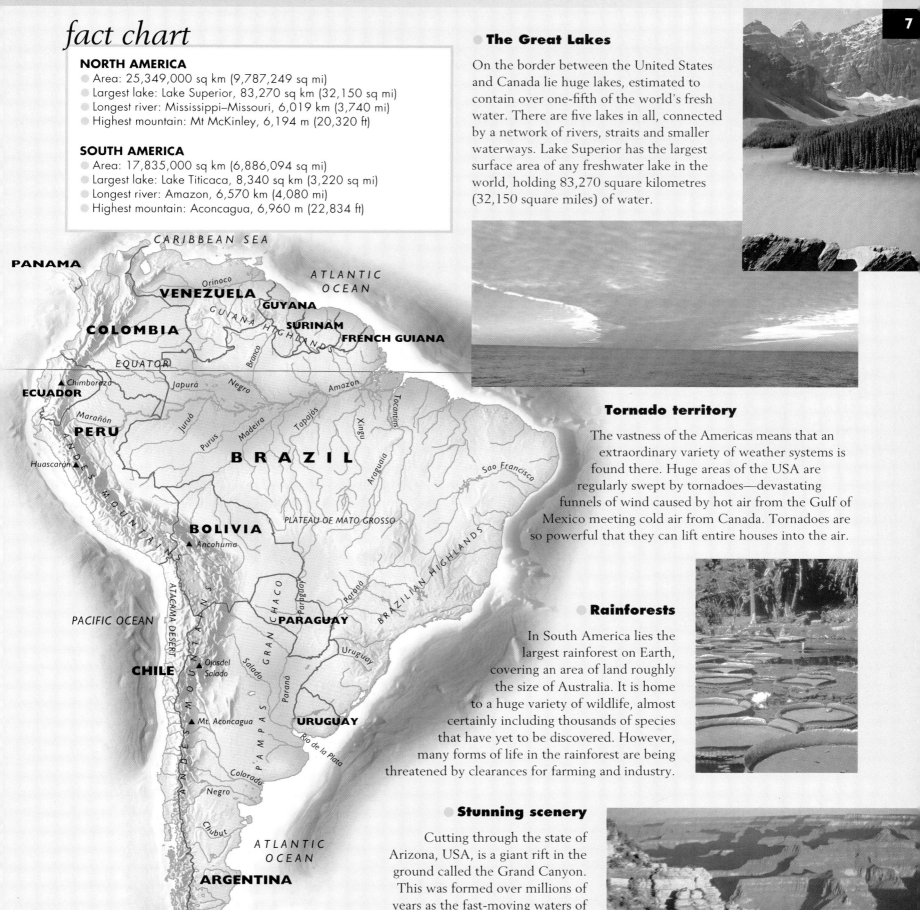

The Great Lakes

On the border between the United States and Canada lie huge lakes, estimated to contain over one-fifth of the world's fresh water. There are five lakes in all, connected by a network of rivers, straits and smaller waterways. Lake Superior has the largest surface area of any freshwater lake in the world, holding 83,270 square kilometres (32,150 square miles) of water.

Tornado territory

The vastness of the Americas means that an extraordinary variety of weather systems is found there. Huge areas of the USA are regularly swept by tornadoes—devastating funnels of wind caused by hot air from the Gulf of Mexico meeting cold air from Canada. Tornadoes are so powerful that they can lift entire houses into the air.

Rainforests

In South America lies the largest rainforest on Earth, covering an area of land roughly the size of Australia. It is home to a huge variety of wildlife, almost certainly including thousands of species that have yet to be discovered. However, many forms of life in the rainforest are being threatened by clearances for farming and industry.

Stunning scenery

Cutting through the state of Arizona, USA, is a giant rift in the ground called the Grand Canyon. This was formed over millions of years as the fast-moving waters of the Colorado River eroded the surrounding rock. It is up to 1.6 kilometres (1 mile) deep in places.

Canada and Alaska

● Sweet exports

The leaf on the Canadian flag is from a maple. Canada produces around three-quarters of the world's maple syrup, which is "tapped" from the trunks of maple trees.

Canada is one of the largest countries in the world, but it has a population of only around 30 million people. Large parts of the north of the country consist of icebound islands and huge lakes, forests and mountains.

Most of Canada's population is in the south, where the climate is milder. Canada has many large cities along its border with the United States of America, including Ottawa, its capital. This was named after the Native American people on whose land the city was built.

Canada has vast natural resources. It is the world's largest exporter of timber and wood products. It also produces large amounts of minerals and metals, including gold, silver, uranium and zinc.

Alaska, to the northwest of Canada, is part of the United States. It is the biggest state, and is one of the world's largest producers of oil, yet has a population of only around half a million people.

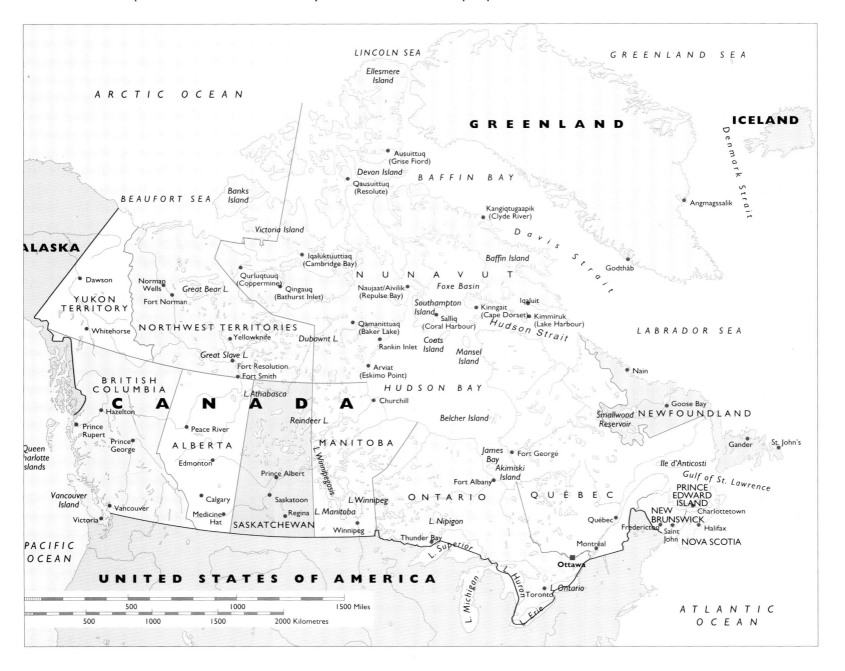

Ice and oil

Conditions in the US state of Alaska can be cold and hostile. However, rich oil deposits have attracted companies and individuals. The Trans-Alaska Pipeline transports oil from northern Alaska to the south of the state.

Wilderness wildlife

Canada's unspoilt regions attract many outdoor enthusiasts. Animals such as moose, wolves and lemmings populate the forests in the centre of the country. Grizzly bears live in the mountains to the west.

Toronto

Toronto is Canada's largest city, with a population of over 3.5 million. It is the country's centre of industry and business but has the lowest crime rate of any city in North America. The CN tower, 553 metres (1,814 feet) high, is the tallest free-standing building in the world today.

fact chart

CANADA
- Area: 9,976,140 sq km (3,851,808 sq mi)
- Population: 30,000,000
- Languages: mainly English and French
- Currency: Canadian dollar

ALASKA
- Area: 1,478,450 sq km (570,833 sq mi)
- Population: 521,000
- Languages: English
- Currency: US dollar

French heritage

Although Canada was part of the British Empire until 1867, French culture has also had a major influence. Montreal, in the province of Quebec, is one of Canada's largest cities, founded by French traders in 1642. Over two-thirds of its inhabitants are French-speakers. French style can also be seen in many of Canada's historic buildings.

Niagara Falls

One of Canada's most visited natural attractions is Niagara Falls, on the border between Canada and the United States. The Niagara River forms the American Falls in the US, and the Horseshoe Falls in Canada. The Horseshoe Falls, 669 metres (2,194 feet) wide and 53 metres (175 feet) high, provide hydroelectric power.

United States of America

The United States of America is one of the most powerful countries in the world. The 50 states have their own governments but send representatives to the national government in the capital, Washington DC. ("DC" stands for the area in which Washington is found: District of Columbia.)

The first wave of European settlers arrived in the sixteenth century, but immigration was greatest in the nineteenth and twentieth centuries. At first settlers stayed fairly near to the East Coast, but gradually they forged further westward. The discovery of gold in California led to the Gold Rush of 1849 and accelerated settlement on the West Coast. Only twenty years later, the railway ran from coast to coast, unifying the country.

The USA has enormous natural resources. Oil, iron and coal are mined in large quantities. The variations in climate mean that produce of all kinds can be farmed, from wheat and cattle in the Midwest to citrus fruit in the Southwest.

The USA has also led the world in many areas of technology. Silicon Valley in California has seen the development of huge advances in computing and communications. The space programme based at Houston in Texas set the first men on the Moon and continues to probe further into the Solar System.

Perhaps the USA's greatest strength comes from its people. Drawn from almost every part of the world, they contribute a rich variety of cultures and outlooks to this vast country.

The 50 stars on the American flag represent the 50 "United States".

Native Americans

Long before Europeans began to settle in the Americas, there were people living there. These Native Americans were named "Indians" by early European explorers who mistakenly thought they had reached the East Indies. In fact, Native Americans had also come from far away. Thousands of years ago, their hunters followed game across an ice bridge between Asia and the Americas. The coming of Europeans changed the way of life of Native Americans for ever.

Harvest in the Midwest

The grain fields of the Midwest stretch as far as the eye can see. Once these were natural prairies, roamed by herds of buffalo. The wheat grown in small European fields could not stand up to the winds of the vast open spaces. It was not until a short, sturdy form of wheat from the steppes of Russia was introduced that America set off on its way to becoming the largest producer of grain in the world.

New York

For most immigrants to America, New York harbour was their first sight of their new homeland. Although New York is not the capital of the USA, it is its largest city and the centre of its financial activity. The heart of New York is Manhattan, a small island once covered by marshes.

South to the sun

The sunny South of the country attracts tourists from all over the world to its beautiful beaches and entertainment centres such as Disney World. Many Americans have also found it an excellent place for their retirement years. But the coast can also suffer from the fearsome power of hurricanes sweeping across the Atlantic Ocean.

fact chart

UNITED STATES OF AMERICA
- Area: 9,372,614 sq km (3,618,794 sq mi)
- Population: 245,871,000
- Languages: English is most widely spoken, but there are a growing number of Spanish speakers and, of course, many other languages have smaller populations
- Currency: US dollar

Hollywood

Long before most people were able to take holidays abroad, they learnt about the USA from films. Hollywood, a suburb of Los Angeles, proved ideal for early film-makers. It had year-round sunshine and was near to locations as varied as mountains, deserts and the ocean. It is still the centre of the American film industry and also has an enormous influence on music and fashion.

On the road

Although the internal combustion engine was invented in Europe and the first cars were made there, it was the American car industry that put motoring within the reach of ordinary people. Henry Ford's factory was the first to use production-line methods to meet the growing demand. Detroit, near the Canadian border, is the centre of the American car industry.

Central America and the Caribbean

A narrow bridge of land joins the two giant continents of North and South America. Central America is formed from seven countries. To the north of these is Mexico, a large land of mountains and forests, deserts and volcanoes, and to the east lies the long chain of islands called the West Indies.

This is an area of enormous geographical variety, ranging from the Mexican desert to the fertile rainforests of Costa Rica and the tropical islands of the Caribbean. People from many ethnic origins inhabit Central America and the Caribbean, contributing to its rich variety of art and culture.

The area also sees extremes of wealth and poverty. There is a great difference between the lifestyles of wealthy tourists and the living conditions of some local people. In the last fifty years, parts of Central America have experienced turmoil involving border disputes and military rule. However, industry continues to develop in this region.

● Stormy weather

The Caribbean islands are idyllic for much of the year, but they are also swept by some of the most powerful weather systems in the world. Ferocious tropical storms called hurricanes can cause devastating damage on the islands between May and October each year. Winds in a hurricane can reach speeds of over 160 km/h (100 mph), creating enormous waves.

● A vital link

Only the Panama Canal divides the continents of North and South America. It was opened in 1914 and provides a vital shipping link between the Atlantic and Pacific Oceans. It is 82 kilometres (51 miles) long and formed from a series of locks. It took forty thousand people ten years to build the canal, sometimes in appallingly difficult conditions.

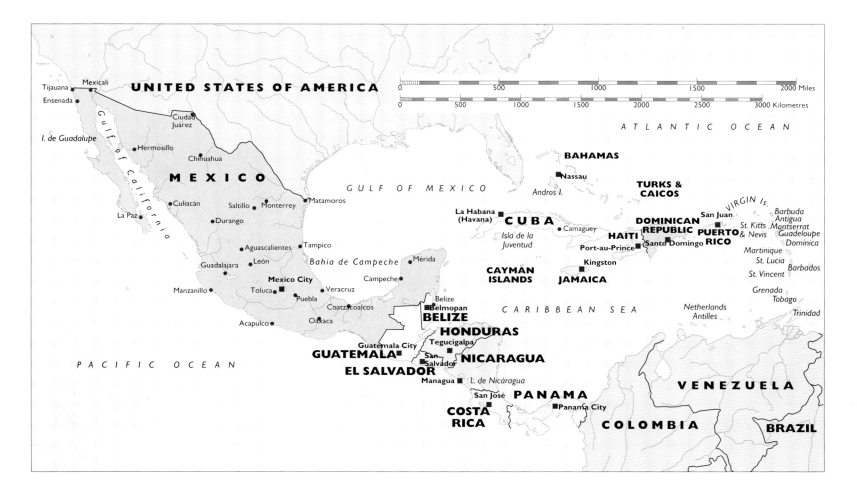

Home of the Aztecs

Mexico contains the world's largest city—Mexico City. It has a population of over twenty million people and is built on the site of the ancient city of Teotihuacan, the capital of the Aztec civilization. Mexico City lies at a very high altitude and is surrounded by mountains. This makes it difficult for exhaust gases from transport and industry to escape, causing problems with air pollution.

Sun-seekers

The beautiful sandy beaches, tropical climate and stunning scenery of the islands of the Caribbean make this area popular for holidays. Thousands of people from Europe and the Americas travel to the West Indies each year, and money from tourism is now vital to the economy of the islands.

Bananas

Bananas, an important crop in many countries of Central America and on many of the Caribbean islands, are exported all over the world. In Honduras, the banana is vital to the country's economy—over sixty per cent of the land is used for cultivating the fruit, and many thousands of people are employed in its harvest.

Cricket

The game of cricket was brought to the West Indies by British travellers in the 1800s, and the West Indies national team is one of the best in the world. Children play the game from their earliest years. The vast, sandy beaches form ideal practice grounds for enthusiasts of all ages.

fact chart

MEXICO
- Area: 1,967,190 sq km (761,604 sq mi)
- Population: 92,000,000
- Languages: Spanish
- Currency: Mexican new peso

GUATEMALA
- Area: 108,890 sq km (42,042 sq mi)
- Population: 10,050,000
- Languages: Spanish
- Currency: Quetzal

BELIZE
- Area: 22,960 sq km (8,866 sq mi)
- Population: 200,000
- Languages: English
- Currency: Belizean dollar

EL SALVADOR
- Area: 21,040 sq km (8,260 sq mi)
- Population: 5,500,000
- Languages: Spanish
- Currency: Colón

HONDURAS
- Area: 112,090 sq km (43,277 sq mi)
- Population: 5,600,000
- Languages: Spanish
- Currency: Lempira

NICARAGUA
- Area: 130,700 sq km (50,463 sq mi)
- Population: 4,200,000
- Languages: Spanish
- Currency: New córdoba

COSTA RICA
- Area: 51,100 sq km (19,652 sq mi)
- Population: 3,300,000
- Languages: Spanish
- Currency: Costa Rican colón

PANAMA
- Area: 77,080 sq km (30,124 sq mi)
- Population: 2,550,000
- Languages: Spanish
- Currency: Balboa

CUBA
- Area: 110,860 sq km (42,803 sq mi)
- Population: 11,000,000
- Languages: Spanish
- Currency: Cuban peso

South America

fact chart

VENEZUELA
- Area: 912,050 sq km (352,140 sq mi)
- Population: 20,220,000
- Languages: Spanish
- Currency: Bolivar

BRAZIL
- Area 8,512,000 sq km (3,286,483 sq mi)
- Population: 150,000,000
- Languages: Portuguese
- Currency: Cruzeiro réal

COLOMBIA
- Area: 1,138,910 sq km (439,737 sq mi)
- Population: 34,000,000
- Languages: Spanish
- Currency: Colombian peso

ECUADOR
- Area: 283,560 sq km (109,480 sq mi)
- Population: 11,200,000
- Languages: Spanish
- Currency: US dollar

PERU
- Area: 1,285,220 sq km (496,230 sq mi)
- Population: 23,000,000
- Languages: Spanish, Quechua and Aymará
- Currency: New sol

BOLIVIA
- Area: 1,098,580 sq km (424,160 sq mi)
- Population: 7,060,000
- Languages: Spanish
- Currency: Boliviano

CHILE
- Area: 736,900 sq km (292,260 sq mi)
- Population: 13,500,000
- Languages: Spanish
- Currency: Chilean peso

PARAGUAY
- Area: 406,750 sq km (157,047 sq mi)
- Population: 4,643,000
- Languages: Spanish
- Currency: Guaraní

URUGUAY
- Area: 177,400 sq km (68,498 sq mi)
- Population: 3,150,000
- Languages: Spanish
- Currency: Uruguayan peso

ARGENTINA
- Area: 2,780,090 sq km (1,073,392 sq mi)
- Population: 34,000,000
- Languages: Spanish
- Currency: Peso

Thirteen countries make up the continent of South America. These range from the enormous nation of Brazil to the narrow, ribbon-like country of Chile that snakes down the west coast.

Northern South America is a region of incredible beauty. The largest rainforest in the world occupies a vast area of Brazil and its neighbouring countries. However, industrial development is encroaching on this region. Farming and oil exploration are also threatening this unique area while fulfilling other economic needs.

Much of South America is rich in natural resources. Large deposits of oil have been discovered in Venezuela, while gold, silver, chrome and iron ore are mined in Guyana.

The Andean region has valuable supplies of precious metals, stones and minerals. Because of the short supply of flat land, crops such as coffee and bananas are grown on terraces that have been cut into the hillsides.

Paraguay, Argentina, Chile and Uruguay make up the southern region of South America. In the centre of Argentina lie the pampas, an enormous fertile plain on which wheat is grown and animals are grazed. Cattle and sheep are farmed in Argentina and Uruguay, while Chile is the world's leading exporter of copper.

● Crucial coffee

Brazil, Columbia, Ecuador and Peru are the world's top coffee exporters. Coffee beans are the seeds of the coffee tree, an evergreen on which green "cherries" ripen to red before splitting to reveal the pairs of seeds inside.

● Easter Island

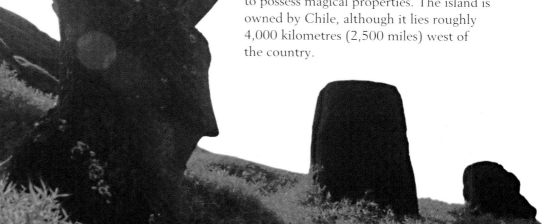

Over 600 of these incredible stone statues were carved by the earliest inhabitants of Easter Island. The carvings were believed to possess magical properties. The island is owned by Chile, although it lies roughly 4,000 kilometres (2,500 miles) west of the country.

CARIBBEAN SEA
Pta. Gallinas

0   500   1000   1500   2000 Miles
0   500   1000   1500   2000   2500   3000 Kilometres

Barranquilla
• Maracaibo • Caracas
PANAMA
COSTA
RICA *Gulf of*
Panama   L. Maracaibo

Medellin

VENEZUELA

ATLANTIC OCEAN

Georgetown
GUYANA Paramaribo
• Bogotá
Cali   **SURINAM** • Cayenne
FRENCH GUIANA
COLOMBIA

Macapá
• Quito
ECUADOR   I. de Marajó
• Guayaquil   • Belém

Manaus   • São Luís
Fortaleza

P E R U   **B R A Z I L**

Recife

• Lima   Maceió

• Cuzco   Salvador
BOLIVIA
L. Titicaca   • Brasília
• La Paz

Arica   L. Poopó

Belo Horizonte

PACIFIC OCEAN

PARAGUAY   São Paulo
CHILE   Asunción   Itaipu Res.   Rio de Janeiro
Antofagasta   Santos

ATLANTIC OCEAN

L. Mar Chiquita   Pôrto Alegre

L. dos Patos

Rosario   L. Mirim
Buenos Aires **URUGUAY**
Santiago • La Plata   Montevideo
ARGENTINA

Bahia Blanca

Golfo San Matias

Isla de Chiloé

Golfo de
San Jorge
Archipelago de
los Chonos   L. Buenos
Aires

Falkland Islands
(Malvinas)

Bahia Grande

Archipelago
Reina Adelaida   Strait of Magellan
Punta Arenas   Tierra del Fuego

South Georgia

Cape Horn   S C O T I A   S E A

Ancient civilizations

In the fifteenth and sixteenth centuries, the powerful Inca Empire dominated the region now known as Peru. The Incas were very skilled in science and technology, building roads and canals throughout their mountainous lands. Today, half of Peru's population can claim descent from the Incas.

Rio de Janeiro

This enormous statue of Christ stands high above the city of Rio de Janeiro. It was the capital of Brazil until it was replaced by the city of Brasilia in 1960. On the outskirts of the city, sprawling slums, called favelas, accommodate the large numbers of people that have travelled here to seek work.

Party time

Brazil is home to a huge variety of cultures. Each year all groups show off their own styles when the famous Brazilian carnival takes to the streets.

Giant wildlife

The Galapagos Islands, lying about 1,000 kilometres (600 miles) from the mainland (west of the map above), are famous as the place where Charles Darwin observed variations in the local wildlife that helped him develop his theory of evolution. The name of the islands comes from the giant tortoises found there.

EUROPE

The coastline of Europe is defined by an irregular series of peninsulas and indentations, and many islands can be found close to the mainland, including the largest group—the British Isles.

Most of Europe lies on a single, colossal plain that stretches from Russia through Germany and southern England down to France. This plain is below sea level in some places. The land here is incredibly fertile and was once covered by thick forests. Most of the trees have now been cleared for farmland. This, plus many abundant resources of coal, gas and oil, have led to the area becoming one of Europe's most densely populated regions.

The most northerly parts of Europe are inside the Arctic Circle. Below this, the large landmass of Scandinavia curves around the Baltic Sea. Mountain ranges, including the Alps and the Pyrennees, separate northern and southern Europe. In the south, the climate is milder, with countries around the Mediterranean having very hot, dry weather during the summer months.

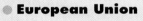

The far west of Europe consists of the Iberian Peninsula. Spain and Portugal occupy this area of land, which is separated from Africa by the narrow Strait of Gibraltar.

European Union

The European Union has grown steadily since it began with six member states. Its aim is to facilitate trade and co-operation between its members. The stars on the EU flag once showed the number of members, but it was decided to stop at twelve!

The Alps

The spectacular mountain range of the Alps divides France and Italy. Its highest mountain is Mont Blanc at 4,807 m (15,771 ft) above sea level. A tunnel through the mountain provides a trade route between France and Italy.

The sunny south

The warmth and sunshine of the countries near the Mediterranean Sea means that a wide variety of crops can be grown, including sunflowers, raised for their seeds. From these, sunflower oil can be pressed. Many parts of this area never experience frost, so tender plants can be grown successfully all year round.

Endangered wildlife

The woodland that used to cover a great deal of Europe once provided habitats for many species of animals and birds. Wolves, for example, were once common in the northern regions of the British Isles and many parts of mainland Europe. Nowadays, they are being reintroduced to parts of Scandinavia, but this is proving a controversial move, with farmers in particular concerned for their livestock.

Underground heat

The island of Iceland, to the northwest of Europe, has more volcanic vents than any other part of the world. Molten rock deep underground heats water and creates hot springs. These are one of the island's main tourist attractions and are used to heat many of its towns.

Europe is the smallest continent in the world after Oceania. It stretches from the Atlantic Ocean in the west to the Ural Mountains in the east, where it borders Asia. The Russian Federation straddles both continents.

fact chart

EUROPE
- Area: 10,490,000 sq km (4,050,189 sq mi)
- Largest Lake: Lake Ladoga, Russian Federation (see page 38), 18,389 sq km (7,100 sq mi)
- Longest river: Volga, 3,530 km (2,194 mi)
- Highest mountain: Mount El'brus, Russian Federation (see page 36), 5,642 m (18,510 ft)

● Ice giants

Much of northern Europe has been shaped by ice. Glaciers are huge rivers of ice that flow very, very slowly, carving deep trenches as they go. The fjords of Norway were made by glaciers during the Ice Age. The ice carved valleys in the rock below sea level. When the ice melted, the sea flooded in.

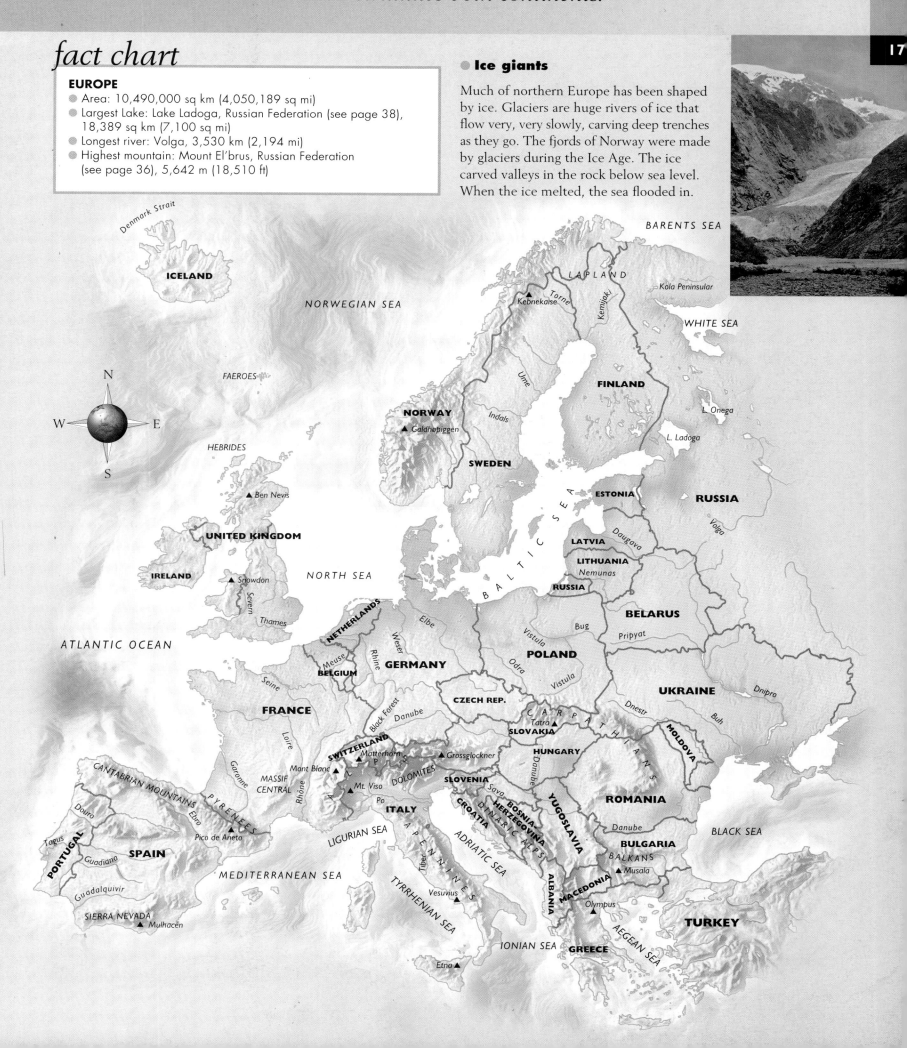

Scandinavia and Finland

The Northern European countries of Norway, Sweden and Denmark are collectively known as Scandinavia. Norway and Sweden form a giant arm that curves around the Baltic Sea. Denmark is the most southerly country in Scandinavia, bordering with north Germany. It includes over a hundred small islands to the east of its mainland.

Mountains, fjords and fast-flowing rivers dominate the landscape of Norway and Sweden. This means that farmland is rare—less than five per cent of the country is suitable for agriculture. Fishing is an important industry and is the reason that most towns in Scandinavia are built on the coast or around lakes.

Inhabitants of Scandinavia enjoy a high standard of living with extensive social welfare programmes. The languages of Denmark, Sweden and Norway are so closely linked that speakers can often understand each other across borders.

Finland shares borders with the Russian Federation and Sweden. For hundreds of years it was ruled by its powerful neighbours but is now the most northerly independent country in the world. The culture and language of Finland varies considerably from its westerly neighbours.

● Adventures on ice

A wooden ski has been found in Sweden that dates back to at least 2500BC. Originally, skis would have been used to help travellers make their way across snowy terrain. Nowadays, tourists ski here for pleasure, and many towns have annual festivals to celebrate the sport.

● Building blocks

Denmark exports one of the most popular toys in the world—Lego. It was invented by a carpenter in the 1930s. The Legoland theme park includes miniature models of many major cities, built from the famous coloured bricks.

● Timber!

Scandinavia and Finland are heavily wooded areas, and forestry has become an important industry. The most common trees in Sweden and Finland are fast-growing pine and spruce. Most of these are cut down and chewed up into pulp from which many different kinds of board and paper are made.

● Shipping industry

The Scandinavian countries and Finland have long been famous for their shipping industry. Beautiful natural harbours around the coast, such as the one in Finland's capital city Helsinki, have allowed ships to be built there for many hundreds of years. Today Norway has one of the world's largest shipping fleets, and many people are employed in the shipping industry.

● Danish bacon

Danish farming is extremely efficient and produces valuable exports. The country produces three times more food than it needs. There are twice as many pigs in Denmark as people!

fact chart

NORWAY
● Area: 323,880 sq km (125,060 sq miles)
● Population: 4,250,000
● Languages: Norwegian
● Currency: Norwegian krone

SWEDEN
● Area: 449,960 sq km (173,730 sq miles)
● Population: 8,585,910
● Languages: Swedish
● Currency: Swedish krona

DENMARK
● Area: 43,070 sq km (16,629 sq miles)
● Population: 5,200,100
● Languages: Danish
● Currency: Danish krone

FINLAND
● Area: 338,130 sq km (130,552 sq miles)
● Population: 4,998,490
● Languages: Finnish and Swedish
● Currency: Euro

● The Norsemen

In the eighth and ninth centuries, Scandinavia was the home of the Vikings. These sea-faring people sailed as far as North America and eastern Russia, establishing colonies and trading posts. They used wooden vessels known as longboats. Their colonization of other countries earned them a reputation for ruthlessness, but the Vikings were also extraordinary craftspeople, artists and storytellers.

The British Isles

The British Isles is a collection of roughly 5,000 islands, separated from mainland Europe by a narrow channel and occupied by two nations called the United Kingdom and the Republic of Ireland. The United Kingdom is a union of the nations of Scotland, England, Wales and Northern Ireland. All four regions of Britain have very strong national identities. In 1997, both Scotland and Wales voted to have their own parliaments. The Republic of Ireland regained its independence in 1921.

Britain has always been a strong agricultural region, with three-quarters of the land used for farming. However, large-scale factory production began here in the 1700s in the Industrial Revolution. Manufacturing techniques originating in Britain are still used widely around the world. Nowadays, many of Britain's traditional industries no longer exist on a large scale. Instead, people are employed in financial and service industries such as banking, education and tourism.

Despite its small size, the United Kingdom has often played a large role in world affairs. The British Empire, which grew and declined between the 1500s and 1900s, covered a huge area of the world and is the reason that English is the main language in many countries worldwide.

● The Swan of Avon

Many great writers and artists have come from the British Isles, including the playwright William Shakespeare. Shakespeare was born in the sixteenth century and wrote numerous plays, including *Hamlet* and *Romeo and Juliet*. Many of his plays were performed in the Globe Theatre in London. The original theatre burned down, but a replica has been built in which Shakespeare's plays are still performed, four hundred years after they were written.

● Playing the game

Team sports have traditionally played an important part in British culture. Many sports, including rugby, cricket, golf and football, were first played in the United Kingdom.

● Historic London

The city of London was founded by the Romans almost two thousand years ago. It is home to many famous historical landmarks. Buildings such as the infamous Tower of London, where many kings and queens have been imprisoned or beheaded, attract millions of visitors each year. In the centre of London is Buckingham Palace, the residence of the royal family.

● Changing industry

Britain's traditional manufacturing industries, producing such items as steel and vehicles, are in decline. However, many overseas companies, attracted by the availability of skilled labour, have opened factories in the country.

● Traditional fuel

In Ireland and Scotland, peat is still dug for fuel and for use as a soil conditioner in gardens. The result of centuries of vegetation becoming compressed, peat is a slow-burning fuel that gives off much less heat than coal or wood. Today, concern over the loss of natural peat bogs and the habitats they provide for wildlife means that alternatives for gardeners are being developed.

fact chart

UNITED KINGDOM
- Area: 244,880 sq km (94,549 sq mi)
- Population: 55,701,000
- Languages: English, Welsh and Gaelic
- Currency: Pound sterling

ENGLAND
- Area: 130,420 sq km (50,355 sq mi)
- Population: 47,536,000

SCOTLAND
- Area: 78,769 sq km (30,412 sq mi)
- Population: 5,094,000

WALES
- Area: 20,767 sq km (8,018 sq mi)
- Population: 2,857,000

NORTHERN IRELAND
- Area: 14,121 sq km (5,452 sq mi)
- Population: 1,578,000

IRELAND
- Area: 70,280 sq km (27,135 sq mi)
- Population: 3,523,450
- Languages: Irish and English
- Currency: Euro

● Black gold

Huge natural reserves beneath the North Sea make oil one of the United Kingdom's most vital sources of income. Enormous offshore oil rigs drill deep into the seabed, piping oil and gas back to the mainland.

France and the Low Countries

France, the largest country in western Europe, has dramatically varied landscapes, ranging from the snow-capped Alps, which separate it from Italy, to the beautiful beaches of its popular south-coast resorts. A vast plain makes up most of northern France, a great deal of which is now farmland. A rail tunnel built under the English Channel in 1994 links France to its neighbour Great Britain.

France is one of Europe's leading farming nations, producing barley, apples, wheat, flax, oats, vegetables and grapes. In the northwest, cattle-farming is widespread, and France is famous for its fine cheeses and wines.

France is also an important industrial nation, manufacturing or processing chemicals, electronics and communications equipment. It is also the base for Arianne, the most successful rocket of the European Space Agency.

The countries to the northeast of France are known as the Low Countries. Belgium, the Netherlands and Luxembourg are part of an economic union called Benelux that encourages trade between the three countries.

Land from the sea

Because it is so low-lying, the Netherlands fights a constant battle against encroachment from the sea. Huge areas of land have been reclaimed by drainage programmes. The fertile land, with its characteristic windmills, produces abundant crops, especially of vegetables and flowers.

On track

France is home to the TGV, one of the world's fastest trains. It runs between Paris and Lyon, and its name is short for *train à grande vitesse*, or "train of great speed". The TGV can reach speeds of over 500 kilometres per hour (310 miles per hour) and has helped to make the French rail system one of the most advanced in the world.

European centres

Brussels, Belgium's capital city, shown above, is home to the administrative centre of the European Union. Luxembourg is a small country, but it plays an important part in international affairs. The headquarters of the European Parliament and the European Court of Justice are sited there.

Cafés and culture

The capital city of Paris is the centre of power in France, and its many attractions make it one of the most visited cities in the world. The Eiffel Tower, built in 1889 to celebrate France's technological success, is 300 metres (984 feet) high.

fact chart

FRANCE
- Area: 551,500 sq km (210,669 sq mi)
- Population: 57,200,000
- Languages: French
- Currency: Euro

MONACO
- Area: 1.95 sq km (0.75 sq mi)
- Population: 28,000
- Languages: French
- Currency: Euro

BELGIUM
- Area: 30,519 sq km (11,783 sq mi)
- Population: 10,200,000
- Languages: Flemish, French and German
- Currency: Euro

NETHERLANDS
- Area: 40,844 sq km (15,769 sq mi)
- Population: 15,500,000
- Languages: Dutch
- Currency: Euro

LUXEMBOURG
- Area: 2,586 sq km (998 sq mi)
- Population: 384,500
- Languages: Luxemburgish
- Currency: Euro

● A principality

To the south of France lies the tiny independent country of Monaco. It has only two towns, Monaco and Monte Carlo. The country is famous for its glamorous image and for its motor racing—both the Monaco Grand Prix and the Monte Carlo Rally are held there. Millions of tourists visit the principality each year, attracted by Monte Carlo's famous casinos. Monaco's harbour, once mainly a fishing port, is now a marina for hundreds of luxury yachts.

● Pioneers of the silver screen

France was one of the first countries to experiment with film. Louis and Auguste Lumière invented the cinema camera and projector in the late nineteenth century. They produced the first ever film in 1895, called *La Sortie des usines Lumière*. The French film industry is now most famous for its highly creative art-house films.

Map scale:
0   50   100   150   200 Miles
0   50   100   150   200   250   300 Kilometres

NORTH SEA

NETHERLANDS
Groningen, Leeuwarden, Sneek, Assen, Emmen, Meppel, Zwolle, Enschede, Haarlem, Amsterdam, Utrecht, Arnhem, The Hague, Rotterdam, Nijmegen, Vlissingen, Breda, Tilburg, Eindhoven, Venlo

BELGIUM
Oostende, Brugge, Gent, Mechelen, Antwerp, Aalst, Leuven, Maastricht, Dunkerque, Kourtijk, Bruxelles, Liège, Verviers, Calais, St.Omer, Lille, Tournai, Charleroi, Huy, Spa, Boulogne, Montreuil, Douai, Mons, Namur, Dinant, Abbeville, Arras, Valenciennes, Cambrai, Bastogne, Amiens, St. Quentin, Libramont

GERMANY

LUXEMBOURG
Luxembourg

UNITED KINGDOM

English Channel

Dieppe, Cherbourg, Baie de la Seine, Fécamp, Montdidier, Le Havre, Bolbec, Rouen, Beauvais, Compiègne, Reims, Verdun, Metz, Channel Islands, Carentan, Lisieux, Elbeuf, Evreux, Mantes-la-Jolie, St. Denis, Meaux, Châlons-sur-Marne, Pont à Mousson, Nancy, Golfe de St-Malo, St. Lô, Caen, Argentan, Paris, Versailles, St.Dizier, Strasbourg, Roscoff, Morlaix, St.-Malo, Granville, Rambouillet, Fontainebleau, Wassy, Toul, Brest, St.-Brieuc, Dinan, Fougeres, Alençon, Chartres, Epinal, Colmar, Douarnenez, Quimper, Pontivy, Rennes, Mayenne, Nemours, Sens, Troyes, Langres, Mulhouse, Vitre, Laval, Le Mans, Orléans, Montargis, Auxerre, Vesoul, Belfort, Lorient, Auray, Vannes, Angers, Blois, Gien, Avallon, Dijon, Besançon, La Chaux de Fonds, St Nazaire, Tours, Vierzon, Dôle, Pontarlier, Belle-Ile, Nantes, Saumur, Châtellerault, Nevers, Autun, Chalon-sur-Saône, Cholet, Bressuire, Châteauroux, Bourges, Le Creusot, Lons le Saunier, La Roche-sur-Yon, Poitiers, La Châtre, Montceau les Mines, Isle d'Yeu, Niort, Moulins, Mâcon, St.Claude, Civray, Montluçon, Lapalisse, Bourg-en-Bresse, Ile de Ré, La Rochelle, Villefranche, Chamonix, Ile d'Oléron, Rochefort, Cognac, Clermont-Ferrand, Lyon, Villeurbanne, Royan, Angoulême, Limoges, Le Mont-Dore, Vienne, Chambéry, Val d'Isère, Lesparre-Médoc, Barbezieux, Nontron, Ambert, St-Étienne, Voiron, Grenoble, Pauillac, Blaye, Périgueux, Tulle, Mauriac, Murat, Yssingeaux, Tournon, Romans-sur-Isère, Bourg, Brive-la-Gaillarde, St. Flour, Le Puy, Valence, Bordeaux, Libourne, Souillac, Aurillac, Arcachon, Bergerac, Figeac, Espalion, Marvejols, Mende, Montélimar, Gap, Marmande, Cahors, Rodez, Florac, Alès, Orange, Carpentras, Mimizan, Villeneuve-sur-Lot, Agen, Villefranche, Le Vigan, Nîmes, Avignon, Apt, Mont-de-Marsan, Castelsarrasin, Montauban, Carmaux, Millau, Arles, Aix-en-Provence, Dax, Gaillac, Albi, Lodève, Montpellier, Draguignan, Nice, Biarritz, Bayonne, Auch, Toulouse, Castres, Mazamet, Sète, Béziers, Marseille, Brignoles, Cannes, St. Jean-de-Luz, Mirande, Muret, Carcassonne, Bandol, Toulon, St.Tropez, Pau, Tarbes, Narbonne, La Seyne-sur-Mer, Lourdes, St. Gaudens, Limoux, Foix, Perpignan, Prades

MONACO

ITALY

SWITZERLAND

SPAIN

ANDORRA

ATLANTIC OCEAN

Bay of Biscay

Golfe de Gascogne

Golfe du Lion

MEDITERRANEAN SEA

Côte d'Azur

Spain and Portugal

The Iberian Peninsula, comprising Spain and Portugal, juts out into the Atlantic from the southwest corner of Europe. It is separated from the continent of Africa by the Strait of Gibraltar. The terrain of the Iberian Peninsula yields few natural resources. A vast, dry, central plain is broken only by mountains. As there is little rain, especially in the centre and south, fertile farmland is in scarce supply.

There are many beautiful beaches, however, and tourism is vital to the economy of the Iberian countries. The Spanish-owned Balearic Islands, which include Majorca, Minorca and Ibiza, are tourist hotspots. Spain also owns the Canary Islands, off the west coast of Africa, which attract thousands of people every year.

Spain was one of Europe's poorest countries until the 1950s, but growing manufacturing industries have vastly expanded the country's economy. Iron ore is mined in the south of the country and used to make steel. Spain is currently one of Europe's largest producers of cars, with major factories in Barcelona and Madrid.

Portugal has an impressive naval history. Vasco da Gama and Ferdinand Magellan, early explorers, were both from Portugal. Nowadays much of Portugal's industry revolves around fishing, tourism and wine producing.

● Surreal architecture

The Spanish city of Barcelona is famous for its magnificent cathedral, designed by the architect Antonio Gaudi. Its many fairytale spires tower above the city below. Work on the cathedral began in 1884, but the building is so intricate that it is still not complete.

● Vibrant cultures

Spain is rich in cultures, traditions and languages. The official language of Spain is Castilian Spanish, but Basque people in the north speak Euskara, a language unrelated to any other European tongue. The Galicians, descended from the Celts, play bagpipes, while the fiery flamenco, which is danced to guitars and castanets, comes from the south.

● Food exports

The climate of Spain makes it an ideal location for growing olives and citrus fruits. Spain is one of the world's leading exporters of mandarins, oranges and lemons. Olives, sunflowers and grapes are also farmed on the mainland, and bananas are grown on the Canary Islands.

● Passing the port

Both Spain and Portugal have flourishing vineyards. Portugal is the home of port, a dark, strong wine often drunk after dinner. It is named after the town of Porto in the northwest of the country. Spain also produces a famous fortified wine, sherry, the name of which comes from the town of Jerez.

fact chart

SPAIN
- Area: 505,992 sq km (195,363 sq mi)
- Population: 39,300,000
- Languages: Spanish
- Currency: Euro

PORTUGAL
- Area: 91,830 sq km (35,455 sq mi)
- Population: 9,860,000
- Languages: Portuguese
- Currency: Euro

● Violent sport

Bullfighting comes from an ancient tradition, going back to Roman spectacles and perhaps further to the Minoan culture. Brightly dressed men and women, named matadors, confront specially bred bulls in the arena. The sport is very popular in Spain but, like many blood sports, it is becoming increasingly controversial internationally.

● The rock of Gibraltar

Gibraltar is a rocky penisula on Spain's southern coast. Standing 426 metres (1,400 feet) above sea level, it once guarded the entrance to the Mediterranean Sea and was a much fought-over location. Gibraltar was captured by the British in 1874, and although Spain claims ownership of the colony, its inhabitants voted to remain part of Britain in 1967.

Italy and Malta

The boot-shaped peninsula of Italy can be found on the southern edge of mainland Europe. At the boot's tip lies the island of Sicily, and further north the island of Sardinia, both of which belong to Italy. The rugged terrain of the Alps carves a line across the north of the country, forming a region of lakes and mountains. A second range of mountains, called the Apennines, runs down the entire length of Italy.

Difficult terrain meant that for centuries this peninsula was divided into many independent states. These states were united under the Romans over two thousand years ago. Then, after they split again in the Middle Ages, rejoined to become Italy as we know it in 1870.

Despite the lack of natural resources in Italy, the country has become one of the most advanced industrial nations in Europe. Italy is a world leader in industrial and product design, importing raw materials and manufacturing goods such as cars, computers, machinery, textiles and chemicals. It is also a major wine-producer.

Halfway between Sicily and North Africa lie the three small islands that form the independent country of Malta. The nation's position in the Mediterranean Sea meant that for many years it was occupied by invading nations. Malta gained independence from Britain in 1964 and now has a strong economy based on shipbuilding and tourism.

● Design centre

Italy has an amazing artistic tradition, with painters and sculptors such as Michelangelo and Leonardo da Vinci flourishing during the period known as the Renaissance. Today, Italy has a worldwide reputation for stylish design, including textiles, clothing, furniture and architecture.

● A feast of food

Italy's wonderful fresh produce, including olive oil, tomatoes, grapes, cheeses and ham, have contributed to a style of cooking that is now popular in many parts of the world. Pasta and pizza can be found in cities as far apart as Canberra and New York.

● Motor passions

Italy is the home of the luxury car industry. Brands such as Ferrari, Lancia and Lamborghini are made in Italy and exported all over the world. Often more expensive than a house, these cars have incredible power and striking designs.

● City of water

Venice, in northern Italy, is a city like no other in the world. Built on a series of islands, the districts of Venice were linked together by a network of hundreds of canals and bridges. The city is now famous for its romantic waterways, and because the narrow streets are unsuitable for cars, floating along the canals is by far the easiest way to travel in the city.

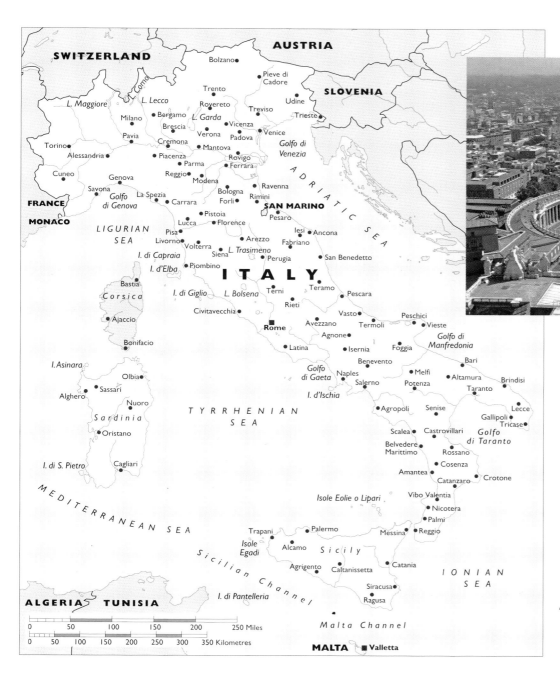

● Separate states

The Vatican City, in Rome, is the world's smallest self-governing country. The home of the Pope, it is also the headquarters of the Roman Catholic Church. Vatican City has its own flag, coins, newspaper and radio station. Further north lies the slightly larger state of San Marino. Despite its size, the national soccer team of this tiny country qualified for the World Cup in 1990.

fact chart

ITALY
- Area: 301,270 sq km (116,321 sq mi)
- Population: 56,411,290
- Languages: Italian
- Currency: Euro

VATICAN CITY
- Area: 0.44 sq km (0.17 sq mi)
- Population: 1,000
- Languages: Italian and Latin
- Currency: Euro

SAN MARINO
- Area: 61 sq km (24 sq mi)
- Population: 21,000
- Languages: Italian
- Currency: Euro

MALTA
- Area: 320 sq km (124 sq mi)
- Population: 400,000
- Languages: Maltese and English
- Currency: Maltese lira

● Ancient Rome

Around 2,000 years ago, the city of Rome was the centre of the mighty Roman Empire. This vast power, which reached its peak in the first century AD, stretched from North Africa to Britain, and from Spain as far west as the Caspian Sea. The remains of colossal monuments can still be seen in Rome, attracting millions of tourists each year. The Coliseum was built as a giant arena in which gladiators fought to the death.

Germany, Switzerland and Austria

Germany lies in the heart of mainland Europe. It is surrounded by nine other countries and has two stretches of coastline to the north. Germany is one of the richest nations in the world, and a leader in the production of cars, electrical goods, chemicals for medicines, and optical instruments.

The Germany that we know today is one of Europe's newest countries. After the Second World War, the country was divided into two nations. East Germany was a communist state. West Germany was a democracy. A wall was built to divide the two, and many people were shot as they tried to cross it. In 1990, the wall was broken down, and Germany became one country again.

To the south of Germany lie the Alps. Occupying this mountainous territory are Switzerland, Liechtenstein and Austria. Switzerland is traditionally neutral and has not taken part in any European war since 1815. As a result, it has a strong economy and is an important financial centre. The tiny country of Liechtenstein has close links with Switzerland.

Austria was once the centre of the Austro-Hungarian Empire that ruled a vast area of central Europe until about 1800. Today, Austria is a heavily industrialized nation, producing large amounts of iron and steel.

● Swiss gold

Swiss banks have a reputation for being secure and discreet. Wealthy people from all over the world choose to store their valuables and money here. No one knows quite how much wealth is stored deep in Swiss vaults.

● Musical capital

Austria's capital city, Vienna, has always been an important cultural centre in Europe, especially for music. Many great composers lived and worked here, including Beethoven, Haydn and Mozart. They travelled to the city to gain aristocratic patrons and win commissions to compose music. Many great musical works were first heard in the impressive Vienna Opera House.

● Eat, drink and be merry

Germany is famous for its hearty food. The *Wurst*, or sausage, is one of the country's most popular foods, with over 1,500 different kinds to choose from. Beer is the national drink of Germany. Each year many different cities hold festivals to celebrate the beverage. The Oktoberfest, held in Munich, is the largest of these celebrations.

● Castles on the Rhine

Germany's history for over a thousand years is vividly portrayed by the many castles that dominate the landscape. Along the banks of the Rhine lie the ruins of vast fortresses that were once used to defend Germany's many independent states. Other castles display the whimsical imagination of wealthy noblemen. Some of Germany's castles remain intact, and their size and splendour make them popular attractions for tourists.

● Snowbound

Switzerland and Austria are famous for winter sports such as skiing and skating, but their spectacular scenery is enjoyed by tourists all year round. Cable cars and ski lifts enable slopes to be climbed and astonishing panoramas to be viewed with minimum effort!

fact chart

GERMANY
● Area: 349,520 sq km (134,950 sq mi)
● Population: 82,000,000
● Languages: German
● Currency: Euro

SWITZERLAND
● Area: 41,290 sq km (15,942 sq mi)
● Population: 6,876,687
● Languages: Romansch, German, Italian and French
● Currency: Swiss franc

AUSTRIA
● Area: 83,850 sq km (32,376 sq mi)
● Population: 7,812,100
● Languages: German
● Currency: Euro

● Industrial strength

The city of Cologne is one of the most important industrial cities in Germany. It is in an area where open-cast mines produce coal and lignite for use in power stations. Germany's plentiful natural resources have helped it to become one of the most important industrial nations in the world.

Eastern Europe

The heart of Europe consists of Poland, the Czech Republic, Slovakia and Hungary. These nations have had a turbulent history. Poland came under Nazi rule in the 1930s and 1940s, and the Czech Republic and Slovakia were, until recently, one country called Czechoslovakia, but split peacefully in 1993. Industry now plays an important part in the economy of this region.

Further east lie the grasslands known as the steppes. Many of the countries in this region were once part of the giant nation that was the USSR (the Union of Soviet Socialist Republics). Until the 1990s, the USSR stretched from central Europe to the Ural Mountains. In 1991, it was split into 15 independent nations. Nine of these are in Europe and six in the continent of Asia.

Large supplies of oil, gas and coal have helped make the Ukraine one of the most powerful regions of the former USSR. To the south of the Ukraine are Romania and Bulgaria. Separated by the River Danube, the countries have many features in common, devoting much of their land to farming.

● Flower power

One of Bulgaria's traditional industries is flower-growing. Each year in June, the village of Kazanluk is home to the Festival of Roses, where people dress in their traditional national costumes and celebrate the many attar roses that are grown in the region. The day after the festival, the rose picking begins. The petals are crushed to produce perfume, which is sold all over the world.

● Polish scientists

Poland has produced many great scientists and thinkers, but two Poles in particular have revolutionized the way that we think about science. In the sixteenth century, the astronomer Nicolaus Copernicus claimed that the Earth revolved around the Sun and was not itself the centre of the universe. In the nineteenth century, Marie Curie pioneered research into radioactivity and named the new element polonium after her birthplace. Today, radiotherapy saves the lives of many cancer patients.

● Grain from Ukraine

Its fertile plains, or steppes, on which are grown wheat, oats and rye, gained the Ukraine the nickname of the "bread-basket of the Soviet Union". Sugar beet and potatoes are also important crops.

fact chart

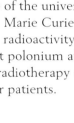

CZECH REPUBLIC
- Area: 78,860 sq km (30,450 sq mi)
- Population: 10,350,000
- Languages: Czech
- Currency: Czech koruna

HUNGARY
- Area: 93,030 sq km (35,919 sq mi)
- Population: 10,300,000
- Languages: Hungarian
- Currency: Forint

ROMANIA
- Area: 237,500 sq km (91,699 sq mi)
- Population: 22,755,000
- Languages: Romanian
- Currency: Leu

BULGARIA
- Area: 110,990 sq km (42,823 sq mi)
- Population: 8,470,000
- Languages: Bulgarian
- Currency: Lev

● Divided capital

Hungary's capital city is known as Budapest but is actually formed from two different cities. Lying on either side of the river Danube are Buda, the old royal capital, and Pest, the more modern centre of finance and politics. Many beautiful historic buildings can be found in Budapest, including the magnificent Houses of Parliament.

A unique heritage

Eastern Europe is becoming an increasingly popular destination for tourists. The stunning scenery of Slovakia's mountainous national parks and the medieval towns of the Czech Republic attract millions of visitors. Many small towns remain much as they did 800 years ago.

Count Dracula

Transylvania, a region of Romania, is the home of vampire legends. The cruelty of Prince Vlad Dracul in the fifteenth century inspired many horrifying tales. Bram Stoker's 1897 novel, *Dracula*, is now perhaps the most famous, leading to further novels and many horror films.

The Balkans

Balkan means "mountain". It is a fitting name for this region. Its daunting mountain ranges include the Carpathians and the Dinaric Alps. The Balkan Peninsula is very wide in the north, stretching from western Slovenia all the way to the Black Sea.

This has always been one of the most unstable parts of Europe, with boundaries between the countries changing frequently. Many of the countries in the Balkans were part of the former Yugoslavia, created in 1918. However, the fall of communism in the 1990s meant that many parts of Yugoslavia declared independence. Fighting between ethnic groups has led to devastating wars and much bloodshed.

Today this region includes Slovenia, Croatia, Bosnia-Herzegovina, the new Yugoslavia, Albania and Macedonia. Because of their location in the centre of Europe, the nations of the Balkans are exceptionally rich in culture and history. Mediterranean, western European and Turkish influences are all present in this area, and there is a great emphasis on creativity and spontaneity. Storytelling, folk dancing and music play a vital part in Balkan culture.

Mountainous terrain means that less than a quarter of the land in the Balkan region is suitable for agriculture. However, fertile river plains yield crops including cabbages, tobacco, maize and chicory. Although natural resources are scarce, industry in the Balkans is rapidly growing and includes production of iron and steel, textiles and footwear, chemicals and wine.

● Eagle country

Albania is locally known as Shqiperi, which translates as "Country of Eagles". Many different kinds of eagle can be seen flying above the rugged, mountainous landscape of the country. The birds can also be seen on the country's flag.

● Danger zone

Many parts of Eastern Europe suffer from pollution. Industrialization has brought both advantages and problems. These trees in Croatia have been devastated by "acid rain". This happens when chemicals from smoke are dissolved in the rain and fall onto the earth below. Only one type of tree has survived.

● Refugees

Unrest in the Balkans has led to hundreds of thousands of ordinary people leaving their homes. Many buildings have been destroyed during fighting. However, there are also huge numbers of people who have fled from "ethnic cleansing". This is when people are persecuted for belonging to a different ethnic origin or religion from those who have gained power. International aid helps homeless families like the ones in Macedonia in the picture above, but it is a huge task.

fact chart

SLOVENIA
- Area: 20,250 sq km (7,819 sq mi)
- Population: 2,000,000
- Languages: Slovenian
- Currency: Tolar

CROATIA
- Area: 56,540 sq km (21,830 sq mi)
- Population: 4,800,000
- Languages: Serbo-Croat
- Currency: Croatian dinar

BOSNIA-HERZEGOVINA
- Area: 51,130 sq km (19,741 sq mi)
- Population: 4,400,000
- Languages: Serbo-Croat
- Currency: New dinar

YUGOSLAVIA
- Area: 102,170 sq km (39,449 sq mi)
- Population: 10,600,000
- Languages: Serbo-Croat
- Currency: Dinar

ALBANIA
- Area: 28,750 sq km (11,100 sq mi)
- Population: 3,360,000
- Languages: Albanian
- Currency: New lek

MACEDONIA
- Area: 25,715 sq km (9,929 sq mi)
- Population: 2,173,000
- Languages: Macedonian
- Currency: Dinar

● **White horses**

Horses have always played a vital part in
the culture of Eastern Europe. The Magyar
people, who invaded Europe in the ninth
century AD, had tough competitions to
exercise their horses and test soldiers'
riding abilities. The country of Slovenia is
still famous for its Lippizaners. These
white horses are considered one of the
finest breeds in the world.

Greece

At the southern tip of the Balkan Peninsula lies Greece. The country is formed from over 2,000 islands, but fewer than 140 are inhabited. Not surprisingly, Greece has always had a strong nautical tradition.

Greece has a fascinating history, with a highly civilized society originating in the city of Athens over 2,500 years ago. Many impressive buildings and statues were created by the ancient Greeks, and they contributed great advances in many areas of culture and technology—from theatre to medicine.

Poor farming conditions and lack of natural resources mean that Greece is one of the poorest members of the European Union, but it is also one of the few countries in the area that has been able to develop relatively peacefully.

Important industries in Greece include concrete manufacturing and shipbuilding, but the country's greatest resource is its warm, sunny weather and fantastic scenery. Tourists experience beautiful surroundings as well as a rich history and culture. Crete, Rhodes and Kos are among the most popular islands. However, there is some concern that sheer numbers of visitors are adversely affecting local ecology.

● Greek mythology

Greek mythology—stories about gods and goddesses who lived on Mount Olympus—strongly influenced Roman mythology and entered the culture of much of Europe. Today most Greeks are Christians or Muslims, but the names of Greek gods live on, such as in the planet Neptune.

● Traditional uniforms

A short period of military service is compulsory in Greece for young men and voluntary for young women. The uniform of the Greek national guards, or *Evzones*, is highly distinctive. It is based on the uniform of the Greek mountain troops who defeated Turkish fighters in 1829 to win independence for Greece.

● The island of Aphrodite

Cyprus is an island off the south coast of Turkey, although since 1974 it has been split into Greek and Turkish parts. Its beautiful beaches and rich cultural heritage have made it a popular tourist destination.

● Green gold

Greece is one of the world's leading producers of olives. These were first grown and exported around 2,500 years ago. The olive oil pressed from the fruit by the Ancient Greeks was considered so valuable that it was traded for gold, jewels and sculptures. Greek olive oil is still exported to countries all around the world.

Riches from the sea

Greece is surrounded by sea on three sides. Its waters contain many kinds of fish and shellfish, which form a key part of the local diet. However, the income of fishermen also depends on tourism, as it is the hotels and tavernas that buy most of their catch.

● Ancient Athens

Athens has been the centre of Greek life for thousands of years. Many famous thinkers, writers and poets lived and worked in the city, including Socrates, whose philosophies are still being taught today. The idea of democracy—where ordinary people have a say in government, rather than a single ruler being totally in control—first began in Athens, although the Athenian interpretation of the term was rather different from ours today. The city was built around the Acropolis, a giant rocky mound on which the ruins of many temples remain.

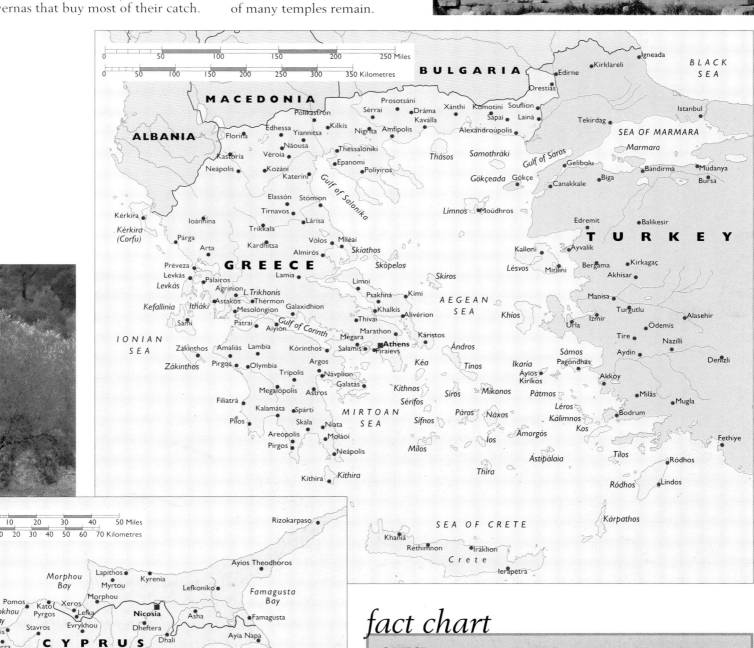

fact chart

GREECE
- Area: 131,990 sq km (50,962 sq mi)
- Population: 10,350,000
- Languages: Greek
- Currency: Euro

ASIA

The Russian Federation dominates the mainland of Asia, stretching from Europe to the Pacific Ocean. To the south lie India, China and the countries of the Middle East. Tens of thousands of islands stretch into the Pacific Ocean. Those that form the countries of Japan, Taiwan and Sri Lanka are situated closest to the mainland. Further out are the many islands of eastern Malaysia, the Philippines, Indonesia and Brunei.

Asia's terrain varies from the icy wastes of the Arctic Circle to the tropical heat of southern India and Sri Lanka. Dense rainforests grow on the many islands of southeast Asia, while lack of rain means that much of central Asia is desert. Some of the world's longest rivers, including the Ganges, can also be found on the continent. When these flood, they deposit rich soil over the surrounding area and create highly fertile plains.

Large parts of the Russian Federation, Mongolia and the Middle East are sparsely populated because of their inhospitable terrain. Despite this, Asia is home to two-thirds of the people in the world, with over forty percent of the world's population living in India and China. The amazing variety of peoples and cultures in Asia stretches back to some of the world's earliest civilizations.

● The top of the world

Two of the world's highest mountain ranges can be found in Asia—the Himalayas and the Karakorams. The Himalayas were formed millions of years ago when the tectonic plate carrying the Indian subcontinent began to press against the mainland of Asia, crumpling the ground to form the dominating mountain range.

KEY	
1 YEMEN	19 BHUTAN
2 OMAN	20 BANGLADESH
3 KUWAIT	21 SRI LANKA
4 JORDAN	22 MYANMAR
5 ISRAEL	23 THAILAND
6 LEBANON	24 LAOS
7 SYRIA	25 VIETNAM
8 IRAQ	26 CAMBODIA
9 ARMENIA	27 MALAYSIA
10 GEORGIA	28 BRUNEI
11 AZERBAIJAN	29 SINGAPORE
12 TURKMENISTAN	30 INDONESIA
13 UZBEKISTAN	31 PHILIPPINES
14 AFGHANISTAN	32 TAIWAN
15 KYRGYZSTAN	33 S. KOREA
16 TAJIKISTAN	34 N. KOREA
17 PAKISTAN	35 JAPAN
18 NEPAL	

Asia covers over thirty percent of the world's land area, making it by far the largest continent, ranging from the Arctic Circle to the Equator.

fact chart

ASIA
- Area: 43,608,000 sq km (16,838,365 sq mi)
- Largest lake: Caspian, 371,000 sq km (143,240 sq mi)
- Longest river: Yangtze, 6,380 km (3,964 mi)
- Highest mountain: Everest, 8,848 m (29,028 ft)

The Dead Sea

Despite its name, the Dead Sea is a large lake on the border between Israel and Jordan. Huge amounts of salt in the water mean that no fish can live there, but mud from the Dead Sea is said by some to be good for human skin! The salt content means that bathers can float effortlessly.

Houses on stilts

Some of the heaviest rains in the world fall in eastern Asia, often causing flooding. In summer, warm air over the water and cooler air over the land causes strong, rain-bearing winds, called monsoons, to blow inland from the ocean. Many houses in this region are built on stilts. These raise the buildings off the ground and prevent living quarters from being flooded.

Gardens of peace

Japanese gardens are famous throughout the world for their air of tranquillity. They are designed to create a peaceful, harmonious landscape in which people can meditate and rest. Some symbolize the larger world, with small bushes and trees representing woods and forests, and rocks representing mountain ranges.

Essential animal

The yak is ideally suited to the bitter cold of the Himalayas. Its thick hair helps it to retain body heat even when the temperature drops below freezing. Some nomadic people in Bhutan and Nepal rely on yaks for an amazing range of necessities, including meat, milk and clothes, and tents made from yak hair. Yaks are also used to carry heavy loads in the mountains, taking food to communities that are cut off when the weather is at its worst.

Asia's wildlife

Asia is home to an extraordinary variety of plants and animals. Peafowl, thought by many to be the most beautiful birds in the world because of the male's stunning tail fan, originated in southern Asia. Not all of Asia's wildlife is so graceful. The Komodo dragon lives on the islands of Indonesia and can often grow to lengths of over three metres (nine feet).

The Russian Federation

Stretching across both Europe and Asia lies the vast landmass of the Russian Federation. It is easily the biggest country in the world, stretching halfway around the globe and covering eight time zones. The most densely populated area of Russia lies in Europe. It is the vast Ural mountain range that is seen as the border between Europe and Asia.

The Russian Federation has had a turbulent past. It was once a great empire ruled by the tsars, until discontent amongst ordinary people led to violent revolutions in 1905 and 1917. A communist state called the Union of Soviet Socialist Republics was established, which lasted until 1990, investing heavily in industry and education. All factories and farms were owned by the government, and it was illegal to run a private business.

When the Soviet Union collapsed, state subsidies came to an end, and the price of food increased dramatically. Food shortages and low incomes across the country caused great hardship. The recent development of service industries and mining has improved matters, but during the long winter months there are still frequent shortages.

Although many parts of the former Soviet Union are now independent countries, the current Russian Federation is still home to over 140 million people. Many of these are employed in the production of coal, iron and steel in the more heavily populated west. Because of the cold climate of Russia, less than ten percent of the land is used for agriculture. Despite this, Russia is the world's leading producer of potatoes, barley, oats and rye.

A nation of dancers

Ballet originated in France, but it was the Russians who made the dance form famous throughout the world. They modified the French style of ballet, adding their own unique movements, positions and rhythms to make it more energetic and exciting. Contemporary Russian ballet companies are still renowned for their passionate dancing and impressive technique.

fact chart

THE RUSSIAN FEDERATION
- Area: 173,750,400 sq km (67,085,029 sq mi)
- Population: 147,021,900
- Languages: Russian
- Currency: Rouble

KAZAKHSTAN
- Area: 2,717,300 sq km (1,049,155 sq mi)
- Population: 16,900,000
- Languages: Kazakh
- Currency: Tenge

UZBEKISTAN
- Area: 447,500 sq km (172,742 sq mi)
- Population: 21,207,000
- Languages: Uzbek
- Currency: Som

The world's longest train journey

The Trans-Siberian railway, built in the early 1900s, stretches from Moscow to Vladivostock. It originally transported political prisoners to penal colonies in Siberia but can now be used to travel across the Russian Federation to reach places such as Mongolia and China. The track is over 9,000 kilometres (5,600 miles) long, and it takes around seven days to travel from one end to the other.

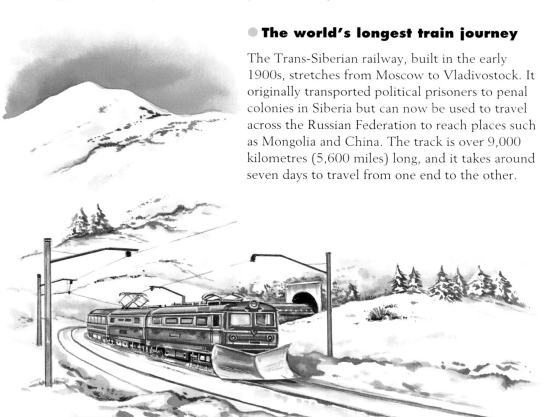

Eastern Russia

The Asian side of the Russian Federation is cold and barren for much of the year—parts of northern Siberia can become colder than the North Pole in the depths of winter. However, this area of Russia has many natural resources. Enormous oilfields and natural gas reserves provide an important source of income for the country, although workers there do have to endure the harsh weather conditions.

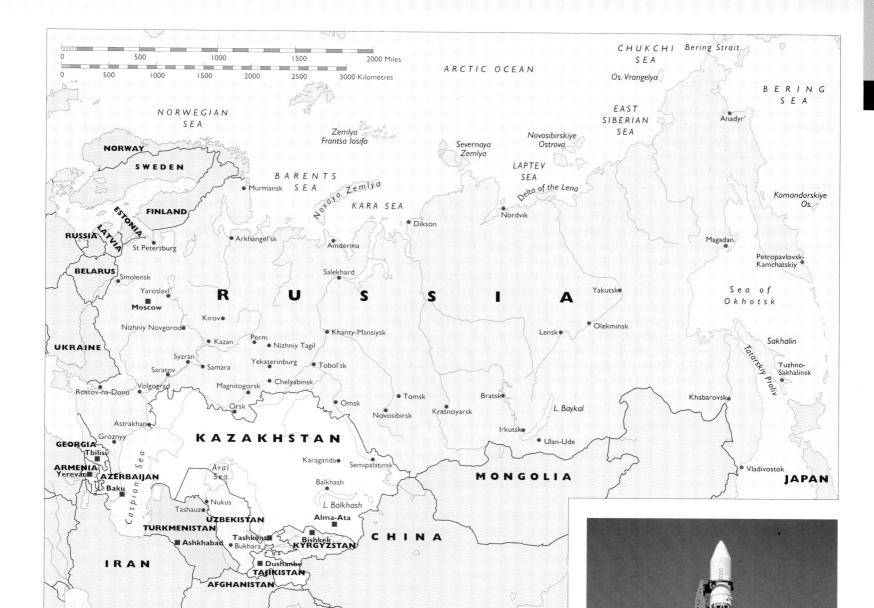

CHUKCHI SEA · Bering Strait
ARCTIC OCEAN
Os. Vrangelya
BERING SEA
Anadyr'
EAST SIBERIAN SEA
NORWEGIAN SEA
Zemlya Frantsa Iosifa
Novosibirskiye Ostrova
LAPTEV SEA
Delta of the Lena
Komandorskiye Os.
NORWAY
SWEDEN
BARENTS SEA
Novaya Zemlya
KARA SEA
Severnaya Zemlya
Magadan
Petropavlovsk-Kamchatskiy
ESTONIA
FINLAND
Murmansk
Dikson
Nordvik
RUSSIA
LATVIA
St Petersburg
Arkhangel'sk
Amderma
Salekhard
Sea of Okhotsk
BELARUS
Smolensk
R U S S I A
Yakutsk
Sakhalin
Yaroslavl'
Moscow
Kirov
Khanty-Mansiysk
Lensk
Olekminsk
Yuzhno-Sakhalinsk
UKRAINE
Nizhniy Novgorod
Perm
Kazan
Nizhniy Tagil
Yekaterinburg
Tobol'sk
Tatarsky Proliv
Khabarovsk
Syzran
Saratov
Samara
Magnitogorsk
Chelyabinsk
Omsk
Tomsk
Bratsk
L. Baykal
Rostov-na-Donu
Volgograd
Orsk
Novosibirsk
Krasnoyarsk
Astrakhan
Groznyy
KAZAKHSTAN
Irkutsk
Ulan-Ude
Vladivostok
JAPAN
GEORGIA
Tbilisi
ARMENIA
Yerevan
AZERBAIJAN
Baku
Caspian Sea
Aral Sea
Karaganda
Semipalatinsk
MONGOLIA
Nukus
Tashauz
Balkhash
L. Balkhash
UZBEKISTAN
Alma-Ata
TURKMENISTAN
Tashkent
Bishkek
CHINA
Ashkhabad
Bukhara
KYRGYZSTAN
IRAN
Dushanbe
TAJIKISTAN
AFGHANISTAN

0 500 1000 1500 2000 Miles
0 500 1000 1500 2000 2500 3000 Kilometres

St Petersburg past and present

St Petersburg is not the capital of the Russian Federation, but it is home to some of the country's most impressive buildings. The enormous Summer and Winter Palaces were built in the eighteenth century as the official residences of the tsars. In 1917, the Winter Palace was stormed by the angry citizens of the city, thus beginning the Russian Revolution. During the communist era, St Petersburg was known as Leningrad, but it later reverted to its former name.

Pioneers of space

The Soviet Union was a pioneering nation in space travel. During the 1950s and 1960s, the USSR competed with the USA to see who could first put a satellite into space. The Soviet Union succeeded when the satellite Sputnik 1 was launched in 1953. The Soviet Union was also the first country to put a man in space when Yuri Gagarin orbited the Earth in 1961.

Southwest Asia

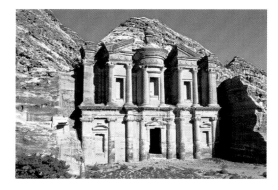

● The rose-red city

Amazing ruins are all that remains of some of the world's earliest civilizations. The city of Petra in Jordan was carved from its rosy rock by the Nabateans in around 400BC.

fact chart

TURKEY
● Area: 779,450 sq km (300,947 sq mi)
● Population: 62,500,000
● Languages: Turkish
● Currency: Turkish lira

SYRIA
● Area: 185,180 sq km (71,498 sq mi)
● Population: 13,500,000
● Languages: Arabic
● Currency: Syrian pound

ISRAEL
● Area: 20,700 sq km (7,992 sq mi)
● Population: 5,500,000
● Languages: Hebrew and Arabic
● Currency: Shekel

JORDAN
● Area: 91,880 sq km (55,433 sq mi)
● Population: 4,450,000
● Languages: Arabic
● Currency: Jordanian dinar

IRAQ
● Area: 438,320 sq km (169,236 sq mi)
● Population: 19,900,000
● Languages: Arabic
● Currency: Iraqi dinar

IRAN
● Area: 1,648,000 sq km (636,296 sq mi)
● Population: 63,000,000
● Languages: Farsi
● Currency: Iranian rial

SAUDI ARABIA
● Area: 2,200,000 sq km (849,420 sq mi)
● Population: 16,000,000
● Languages: Arabic
● Currency: Saudi riyal

Often called the Middle East, southwest Asia is a collection of fifteen varied countries. The nation of Turkey straddles both Europe and Asia, and was the centre of the mighty Ottoman Empire in the 1400s. On the Mediterranean coast lie the nations of Syria, Lebanon and Israel, each of great significance to major world religions.

Further east lies the desert terrain of Jordan, Saudi Arabia, Yemen and Oman. Many areas of these counties are thinly populated because of the lack of water and farmland. The mountainous regions of Iraq and Iran lie to the north.

Several smaller countries also occupy the Middle East. Kuwait lies to the south of Iraq, and the peninsula of Qatar stretches out into the Persian Gulf. Above this sits the small island chain of Bahrain.

The barren, sandy expanse of the Arab Emirates lies on the shores of the Mediterranean. This was once a region of separate Arab states, each ruled by a different prince. The discovery of oil led to the separate states joining together in 1970.

● Behind the veil

In some Islamic countries, the roles of men and women are clearly defined. Women may wear veils, covering everything except their eyes. There is a tradition in this part of the world (and others) of men and women having separate living quarters. To some people, this appears restrictive. Others feel that clear roles offer freedom to both sexes.

● The oil wars

The discovery of oil in the Middle East has made it a very wealthy part of the world. However, it has also heightened tension between countries in this area, leading to violent clashes. In 1990, Iraq invaded Kuwait. During the Gulf War that followed, Iraq set fire to many of Kuwait's oil wells. Kuwait was freed by a multinational force in 1991.

● Religious centres

Three ancient religions have their roots in southwest Asia. Judaism, Christianity and Islam all developed here and gradually spread worldwide. As elsewhere in the world, religious differences have meant that in the past and still today this can be an area of violent conflict. Jerusalem, in Israel, is an important holy place for all three faiths. The Dome of the Rock, which is sacred to Muslims, and the Western Wall, which is sacred to Jews, are only two of the many religious sites in this busy city.

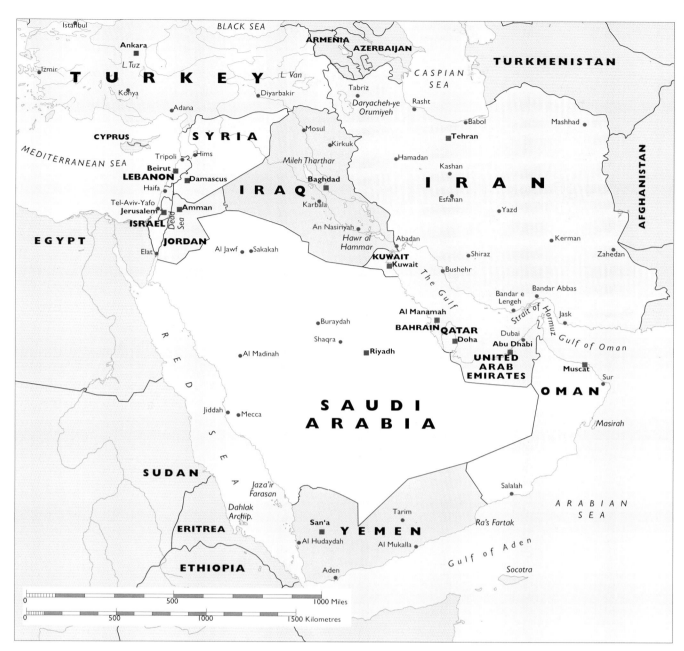

ARMENIA AZERBAIJAN
Istanbul
Ankara
L. Tuz
TURKEY
TURKMENISTAN
Izmir
L. Van
CASPIAN
SEA
Konya
Diyarbakir
Tabriz
Daryacheh-ye
Orumiyeh
Rasht
CYPRUS
SYRIA
Adana
Babol
Mashhad
Mosul
Tehran
IRAN
MEDITERRANEAN SEA
Tripoli
Hims
Kirkuk
Mileh Tharthar
Hamadan
Kashan
Beirut
LEBANON
Damascus
Baghdad
AFGHANISTAN
Haifa
Esfahan
Tel-Aviv-Yafo
IRAQ
Karbala
Yazd
Amman
Jerusalem
Dead Sea
An Nasiriyah
ISRAEL
Abadan
Kerman
EGYPT
JORDAN
Hawr al
Hammar
Shiraz
Zahedan
Elat
Al Jawf
Sakakah
KUWAIT
Kuwait
Bushehr
Bandar Abbas
RED
Bandar e
Lengeh
Strait of Hormuz
Jask
Buraydah
Al Manamah
Dubai
Gulf of Oman
SEA
Shaqra
BAHRAIN QATAR
Abu Dhabi
Al Madinah
Riyadh
Doha
Muscat
Sur
UNITED
ARAB
EMIRATES
OMAN
Jiddah
Mecca
SAUDI
ARABIA
Masirah
SUDAN
Jaza'ir
Farasan
ARABIAN
SEA
Salalah
Dahlak
Archip.
Tarim
ERITREA
San'a
YEMEN
Ra's Fartak
Al Hudaydah
Al Mukalla
ETHIOPIA
Aden
Gulf of Aden
Socotra

The Gulf

| 0 | 500 | 1000 Miles |
| 0 | 500 | 1000 | 1500 Kilometres |

Ships of the desert

Large areas of the Middle East are covered by desert. This terrain is difficult to cross on foot, and modern cars often cannot cope with the intense heat. Some people still use camels to cross the desert. These creatures have adapted to desert conditions and can travel for long distances without water. Because of this, they have been called the "ships of the desert".

Farming in the desert

An aerial view of southwest Asia shows a stark difference between river valleys, where there is plentiful vegetation, and barren desert areas that have no source of water. Irrigation has enabled formerly infertile areas to be farmed, with watered areas clearly visible from the air.

Southern Asia

Over one fifth of the world's population lives on a giant peninsula of land that juts out into the Indian Ocean. The area is so huge that it is often called the Indian subcontinent, including the countries of Pakistan, Bangladesh, Afghanistan, Nepal, Bhutan and Sri Lanka, as well as India. It is a region of contrasts, with deserts, tropical beaches and the Himalayan mountain range as well as fertile land.

Much of India's land is used for farming, with over half the population living in rural areas. Crops such as rice, cotton, fruit, vegetables, tea and coffee are widely grown. India's busy cities are home to flourishing manufacturing industries, with new technology also a growing sector.

The countries of Nepal and Bhutan lie deep in the Himalayas. Nepal encourages tourism, but Bhutan's traditions often prevent visitors from entering the country. It is illegal not to wear Bhutan's traditional dress, and television is banned.

Wildlife in danger

Many amazing species of animal live on the Indian subcontinent, including tigers, elephants and rhinoceroses. However, many of these animals are being threatened by poachers and urban expansion. Countries such as India and Nepal are setting up reserves to protect their rarest species.

Rice fields

Rice is the staple food for over half the Earth's population. It was first grown in south Asia, and over a fifth of the world's rice harvest comes from India. Rice is grown in paddy fields, which are flooded before the shoots are planted.

The holy river

Stretching across the north of India is the Ganges River, believed by Hindus to be sacred. Varanasi, which lies on the banks of the Ganges, is the holiest of Hindu cities. Millions of people visit it each year. Many bathe in or drink the waters of the Ganges, believing that by doing so their sins will be washed away.

Poverty

Many factors contribute to the poverty of large numbers of people in southern Asia. The size of the population in countries such as India makes developing welfare systems a massive task. Violent conflicts have also caused homelessness. A civil war in Afghanistan in the 1980s led to the country becoming one of the poorest in the world. In other parts of southern Asia, disputes over territories, such as the disagreement between Pakistan and India over the region of Kashmir, continue to lead to violence.

fact chart

INDIA
- Area: 3,287,590sq km (1,269,345 sq mi)
- Population: 945,121,000
- Languages: Hindi, English
- Currency: Indian rupee

PAKISTAN
- Area: 796,095 sq km (307,376 sq mi)
- Population: 133,510,000
- Languages: Urdu
- Currency: Pakistani rupee

NEPAL
- Area: 147,180 sq km (54,599 sq mi)
- Population: 21,100,000
- Languages: Nepali
- Currency: Nepalese rupee

AFGHANISTAN
- Area: 652,090 sq km (251,773 sq mi)
- Population: 24,167,000
- Languages: Persian, Pashtu
- Currency: Afghani

SRI LANKA
- Area: 65,610 sq km (25,332 sq mi)
- Population: 18,502,000
- Languages: Sinhalese and Tamil
- Currency: Sri Lankan rupee

Hinduism

Like the Buddhist and Sikh religions, the Hindu faith originated in India. Hinduism has many gods and goddesses, representing different forces and aspects of life. Traditionally, the faith incorporates a caste system and the idea of reincarnation, where a person's social position depends on how he or she acted in a previous life. The festival of Holi is a time of merry-making, when these differences in position are, for once, forgotten.

Taj Mahal

Sometimes described as the most beautiful building on Earth, the Taj Mahal is in fact a tomb for the wife of Shah Jahan, a Mughal emperor. It was completed in 1653 and lies close to the city of Agra in India. Its many domes and pillars are made of solid white marble, and its beauty has made it one of India's most visited tourist attractions.

China

China has more people than any other country. Farming is a vital part of its economy, with China being the world's leading exporter of rice and tobacco. Although vast areas of China are mountainous or deserts, parts of the south have a tropical climate.

China is also becoming increasingly industrialized. Enormous cities have grown up next to fertile river plains, and cheap labour in factories has led to many western companies manufacturing there.

For 2,500 years, China was a powerful empire with trading routes that stretched across the world. The invention and first manufacture of silk cloth, paper and gunpowder are all said to have taken place in China. Civil unrest in the 1900s led eventually to a communist regime being established in 1948.

One of China's biggest challenges is population control. For many years families have been forcefully urged to have only one child.

To the north of China lies Mongolia. Once the centre of a vast empire, it has recently begun to harvest its important reserves of oil and coal. The Tibetan Autonomous Region has been part of China since the 1950s. Many people want Tibet to return to its status as an independent country.

fact chart

CHINA
- Area: 9,396,960 sq km (3,705,405 sq mi)
- Population: 1,133,682,501
- Languages: Mandarin Chinese
- Currency: Yuan

MONGOLIA
- Area: 1,565,000 sq km (604,250 sq mi)
- Population: 2,043,400
- Languages: Mongolian
- Currency: Tughrik

HONG KONG
- Area: 1,045 sq km (403 sq mi)
- Population: 5,674,114
- Languages: English, Cantonese Chinese
- Currency: Hong Kong dollar

TAIWAN
- Area: 36,179 sq km (13,969 sq mi)
- Population: 20,800,000
- Languages: Mandarin Chinese
- Currency: New Taiwan dollar

● Chinese myths

The dragon, symbolizing strength and wisdom, plays an important part in the mythology and culture of China. At Chinese New Year celebrations, giant dragons made from paper and cloth are paraded through the streets for good luck.

● Disciplined defence

China is the birthplace of many different kinds of martial arts, disciplined forms of exercise that are also methods of self-defence. Forms such as kung fu and kick-boxing have been made popular around the world by Hollywood film stars such as Bruce Lee.

● Buddhism

The religion of Buddhism is of great importance in East Asia. It was developed around 500BC by a Nepalese-born prince who gave up his luxurious lifestyle in order to seek enlightenment. He called himself Buddha, which means "to be enlightened". Buddhists believe that suffering is caused by desiring things and sensations. Images of the Buddha often show a seated figure with a serene, almost feminine face.

● The Great Wall

China boasts the oldest man-made structure that can be seen from space. The Great Wall of China was built over 2,200 years ago to help defend China's northern borders against invading Mongols. Incredibly, the wall stretches for over 6,000 kilometres (3,700 miles)! It is now a major tourist attraction.

RUSSIA

Qiqihar

Harbin
Mudanjiang

Choybalsan
Tamsagbulag
Changchun
Jilin

Hovsgol
Nuur

Ulaangom

■ Ulaanbaatar

Tonghua

MONGOLIA

Shenyang
Fushun
N. KOREA

KAZAKHSTAN

Fuhai

Hovd

Chifeng
Jinzhou
Anshan

S. KOREA

Ebinur Hu
Karamay

Korea
Bay

Kuytun

Dalandzadgad

Beijing
Dalian
Weihai

Yining

Baotou
Tianjin

Yantai

KYRGYZSTAN

Ürümqi

Hami

Shizuishan

YELLOW
SEA

Bosten Hu

Shijiazhuang
Zibo
Qingdao

Aksu

Yumen

Yinchuan
Taiyuan
Jinan

Taitema Hu

Weishan Hu
Gaoyou Hu

Xuzhou

Hotan

Qinghai Hu

Xining

Zhengzhou
Hongze Hu
Nantong

Lanzhou
Nanjing
Tai Hu
Shanghai

Chao Hu

Gyaring
Hu

Xi'an

Hangzhou
Shaoxing

Ngoring
Hu

INDIA

Wuhan

CHINA

Yichang

Poyang Hu
Wenzhou

Siling Co

Dongting Hu

Nanchang

Qamdo

Chengdu

Changsha

Fuzhou

Tangra
Yumco

Nam Co

Chongqing

Leshan
Luzhou

Hengyang

Zhangzhou

NEPAL

Lhasa

Xiaguan

Guiyang

Xiamen

Xigaze

Shantou

BHUTAN

Kunming

Liuzhou

Guangzhou

Hong Kong
Macao

MYANMAR

Gejiu

Nanning

Pingxiang
Zhanjiang

VIETNAM

SOUTH
CHINA
SEA

LAOS

Haikou

Gulf of
Tongkin

Hainan

Scale:
0 — 500 — 1000 Miles
0 — 500 — 1000 — 1500 Kilometres

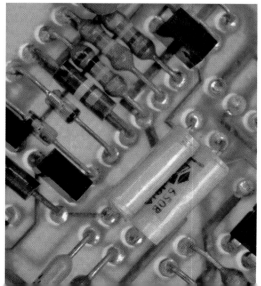

● Hong Kong

Hong Kong is a collection of 235 islands and a section of mainland China called Kowloon. Leased to Britain in 1841, this important trading port returned to Chinese rule in 1997.

● Electronics

The island of Taiwan has few natural resources and for many hundreds of years was a poor region with an economy based on agriculture. Recently, however, Taiwan has earned a worldwide reputation for its manufacturing industry, including the production of electrical and electronic goods. Income from its export of televisions and textiles has enabled the island to import all the materials it needs to become one of the world's leading industrial economies.

Southeast Asia

A large peninsula of land jutting out from India and China forms the mainland of southeast Asia, including the countries of Laos, Thailand, Cambodia, Vietnam and Myanmar—formerly known as Burma. Although there are many natural resources in this area, bitter civil wars in many of the countries has prevented industry from developing. A military dictatorship in Burma beginning in the 1940s led the country to be isolated from the rest of the world. In Vietnam, a civil war in the 1960s and 1970s devastated the country's economy.

Tens of thousands of islands lying off the coast of the mainland make up the rest of southeast Asia. Closest to the peninsula is Singapore, a country made up of over 50 islands. This is one of the wealthiest countries in Asia, with an economy based on banking, trade and electronics. Further out lie the islands that make up Brunei, Indonesia, the Philippines and eastern Malaysia. Abundant reserves of oil in Brunei have led to its sultan becoming the richest ruler in the world.

● Elephant power

Elephants have always been an important part of the culture of Laos. The country was originally known as "The Kingdom of a Million Elephants", and the giant creatures were used by military leaders to crush opposing armies. Nowadays, elephants are employed in the logging industry. Their incredible strength can help fell large trees and then move the trunks to be processed.

Off the east coast of China lies Japan, which consists of over 3,000 islands. Agricultural land is sparse, but Japan is a world leader in the production of electrical goods. In the far east of Asia are the mountainous countries of North and South Korea. South Korea has one of the world's fastest growing economies, producing computers and electrical goods.

fact chart

JAPAN
- Area: 369,700 sq km (142,742 sq mi)
- Population: 126,300,000
- Languages: Japanese
- Currency: Yen

VIETNAM
- Area: 329,560 sq km (127,244 sq mi)
- Population: 71,000,000
- Languages: Vietnamese
- Currency: Dong

MALAYSIA
- Area: 329,750 sq km (127,317 sq mi)
- Population: 20,500,000
- Languages: Bahasa Malaysia
- Currency: Malaysian dollar (ringgit)

SINGAPORE
- Area: 640 sq km (247 sq mi)
- Population: 2,800,000
- Languages: English, Mandarin, Tamil and Malay
- Currency: Singaporean dollar

INDONESIA
- Area: 1,904,570 sq km (735,358 sq mi)
- Population: 190,000,000
- Languages: Bahasa Indonesia
- Currency: Rupiah

● Sticky stuff

The climate of many parts of southeast Asia is perfect for growing rubber trees. Their trunks are cut to enable the milky sap, called latex, to drip out. This sticky liquid is then processed to become rubber that can be used in tyres and a range of other goods.

● Rubies

The riverbeds of Myanmar and Thailand sometimes conceal small shards of the beautiful red jewel called the ruby. Local farmers pan for rubies in the hope of a little extra income. They use wooden sieves to dredge the gravel at the bottom of the river. Rubies are rarely found, but large gems can sell for huge amounts of money.

● Terraced fields

Because fertile ground is often in short supply in southeast Asia, every last metre of land is modified for farming. Many of the region's hills have had step-like terraces dug into them to allow extra crops to be grown. The steps prevent fertile soil from being washed away by rainwater.

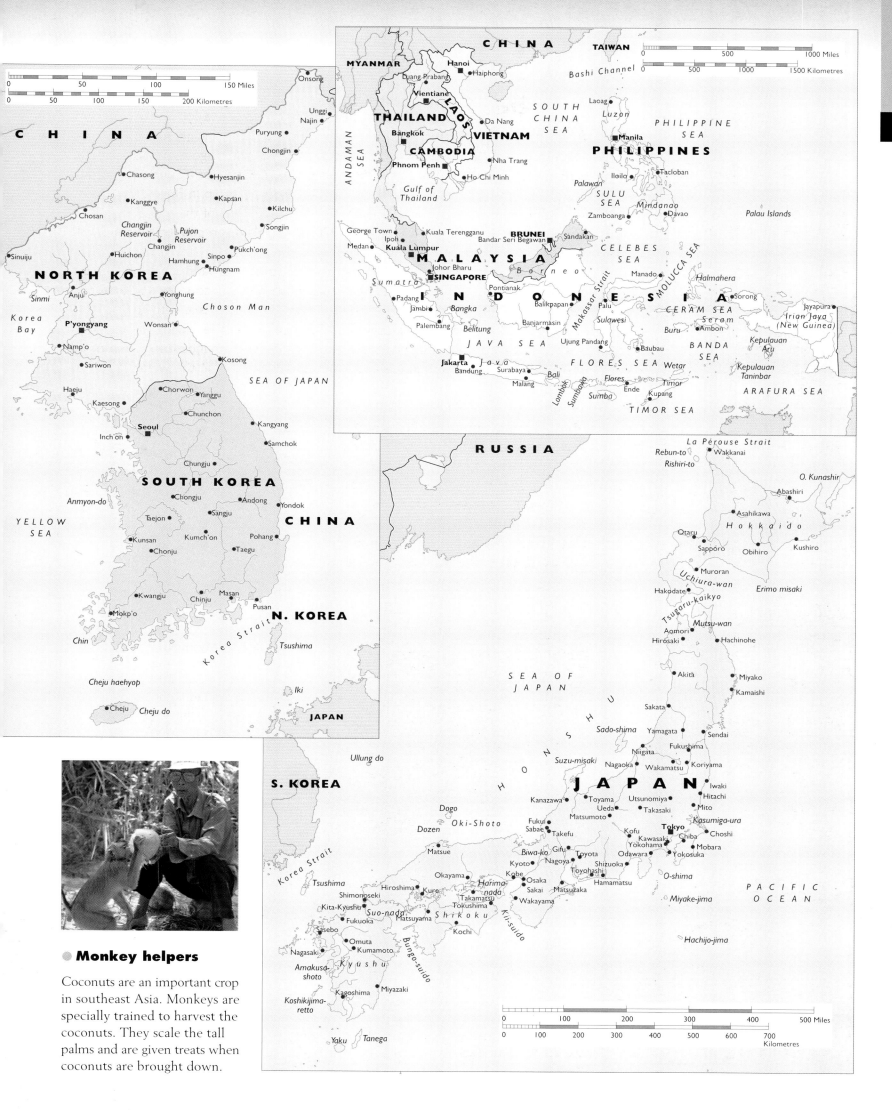

● Monkey helpers

Coconuts are an important crop in southeast Asia. Monkeys are specially trained to harvest the coconuts. They scale the tall palms and are given treats when coconuts are brought down.

AFRICA

Most of the African continent is made up of a large plateau, broken up by several mountain ranges and surrounded in many places by narrow coastal plains. Dry grasslands called savannah can be found north and south of the equator. Rainfall here comes only once a year, but the plant and animal life of the region has adapted to survive in the dry climate. To the extreme north and south of the continent lie several desert regions.

East Africa is marked by an enormous scar. A huge crack in the Earth's crust has produced a dramatic landscape of volcanoes, gorges and enormous lakes. This region is known as the Great Rift Valley. It stretches from Mozambique all the way north to Syria, in Asia. Some scientists believe that the lands to the east of the Great Rift will eventually break away from the mainland of Africa, forming a separate continent.

Approximately 400 kilometres (250 miles) to the east of Central Africa lies the island of Madagascar. This is the fourth largest island in the world. It separated from the African mainland over 150 million years ago, and is home to hundreds of living things that can be found nowhere else on Earth, such as the ringtail lemur.

Savannah wildlife

On the savannah of East Africa, golden grass and sparse trees provide a unique environment for many species of animal and bird. Herds of elephants, zebras and giraffes live there, frequently on the move in search of water and fresh grass. Predators such as lions and cheetahs also flourish, hunting in groups among the vulnerable grazing animals.

Life in the Sahara

The arid, barren landscape of the Sahara Desert means that only specially adapted plants and animals can live there. The world's highest temperature in the shade, 58°C (136°F), was recorded in the Sahara, but at night temperatures in the desert can often drop below freezing.

Victoria Falls

One of the most impressive sights in Africa is that of the Zambezi River plummeting over an 128-metre (420-foot) cliff face to form the Victoria Falls. This waterfall lies between Zambia and Zimbabwe, and the mist and thunderous noise produced by the falling water can be seen and heard many miles away.

Mighty rivers

Africa is drained by several of the world's largest rivers. These include the Nile, which is 6,738 kilometres (4,187 miles) long, and the Niger, which drains a basin over three times the size of France. These rivers cut through some of the driest regions on the continent, providing a vital lifeline for plants, animals and humans.

Africa is the world's second largest continent. Snow is only ever found on the peaks of mountains, but heat, heavy rainfall and tropical storms are more common, and dense rainforests flourish around the equator.

fact chart

AFRICA
Area: 30,335,000 sq km (11,712,434 sq mi)
Largest lake: Lake Victoria, 68,800 sq km (32,150 sq mi)
Longest river: Nile, 6,738 km (4,187 mi)
Highest mountain: Kilimanjaro, 5,895 m (19,341 ft)

Mount Kilimanjaro

At the southern tip of the Great Rift Valley lies Africa's tallest mountain. Mount Kilimanjaro towers above the flat savannah below. Its steep sides are characteristic of the Great Rift Valley, which was formed when enormous areas of land sank between faults in the Earth's crust millions of years ago.

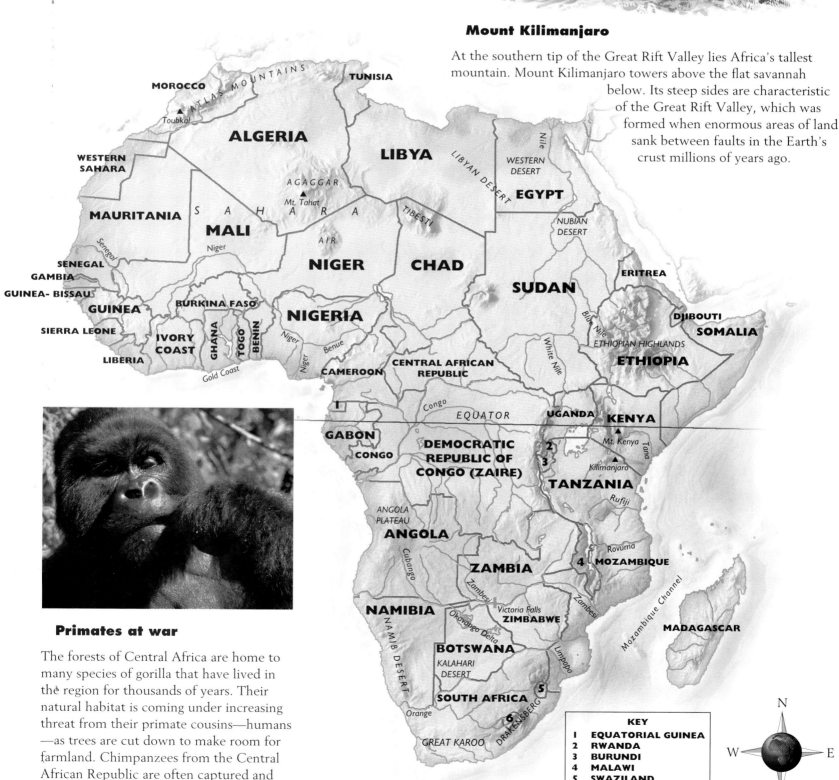

Primates at war

The forests of Central Africa are home to many species of gorilla that have lived in the region for thousands of years. Their natural habitat is coming under increasing threat from their primate cousins—humans —as trees are cut down to make room for farmland. Chimpanzees from the Central African Republic are often captured and sold to zoos and research laboratories.

KEY
1 EQUATORIAL GUINEA
2 RWANDA
3 BURUNDI
4 MALAWI
5 SWAZILAND
6 LESOTHO

North Africa

Plant crops

Egypt produces over one third of the world's cotton, which grows on small bushes that need warmth for the cotton bolls to develop. Morocco produces thousands of tonnes of roses, carnations and marigolds, as well as the valuable spice saffron, used to flavour rice.

fact chart

MOROCCO
Area: 458,730 sq km (177,115 sq mi)
Population: 28,500,000
Languages: Arabic
Currency: Moroccan dirham

ALGERIA
Area: 2,381,740 sq km (919,594 sq mi)
Population: 27,100,000
Languages: Arabic
Currency: Algerian dinar

LIBYA
Area: 1,759,540 sq km (679,362 sq mi)
Population: 5,650,000
Languages: Arabic
Currency: Libyan dinar

EGYPT
Area: 1,001,450 sq km (386,662 sq mi)
Population: 56,500,000
Languages: Arabic
Currency: Egyptian pound

NIGERIA
Area: 923,770 sq km (356,669 sq mi)
Population: 120,000,000
Languages: English
Currency: Naira

SIERRA LEONE
Area: 73,330 sq km (28,311 sq mi)
Population: 4,500,000
Languages: English
Currency: Leone

ETHIOPIA
Area: 1,157,600 sq km (446,949 sq mi)
Population: 55,000,000
Languages: Amharic
Currency: Ethiopian birr

The vast, dry terrain of the Sahara Desert stretches over three-fifths of North Africa and is almost as big as the entire United States of America. North Africa is largely flat, with only the Ethiopian Highlands in the east and the Atlas Mountains in the north rising above the low plateau.

Fourteen independent countries occupy North Africa, ranging from the monarchy of Morocco in the west, which is a popular tourist destination, to the poverty stricken eastern countries of Ethiopia and Eritrea.

Many countries of North Africa are very poor, and industry is scarce. Farming, however, is important and employs over half of North Africa's population. The export of goods such as citrus fruits from Tunisia and coffee from Ethiopia is vital to the economy of the region. Recent talks between Africa and wealthier countries around the world have led to some national debts being cancelled, allowing the countries of Africa to develop more swiftly.

Massive monuments

Northwest Africa was the centre of one of the world's oldest and greatest civilizations. The Egyptian Empire developed in the Nile Valley over five thousand years ago, trading with countries around the Mediterranean Sea. The ancient Egyptians were incredibly advanced in medicine, science and astronomy. They also constructed vast temples and monuments. The pyramids of Egypt are giant tombs in which the pharaohs (kings) of the ancient Egyptians were buried.

Moroccan horsemen

Many years ago, the Moors of Morocco were famous for their riding skills and had a fierce army that fought on horseback. The people of Morocco enjoy traditional demonstrations of horsemanship. Fast and dangerous displays called fantasias are regularly held.

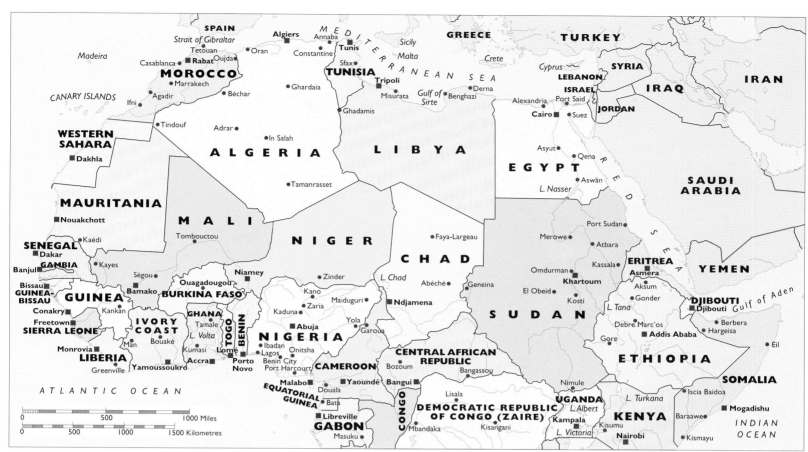

New industry

Some parts of North Africa have abundant natural resources deep underground. Morocco lies over nearly three-quarters of the world's phosphate supply, the mining of which is vital to the country's economy. Giant factories convert the phosphates into fertilizers and other chemicals that are then exported all over the world.

Nomads of the desert

Although the deserts of Africa are largely inhospitable, some groups of people have lived there for centuries. The Tuareg and Bedouin peoples are nomads. For centuries, they have roamed the desert lands, trading and seeking the sparse areas of vegetation to feed and water their animals. Recently, severe drought has devastated much of the land surrounding the deserts, forcing many nomadic people to abandon their traditional way of life.

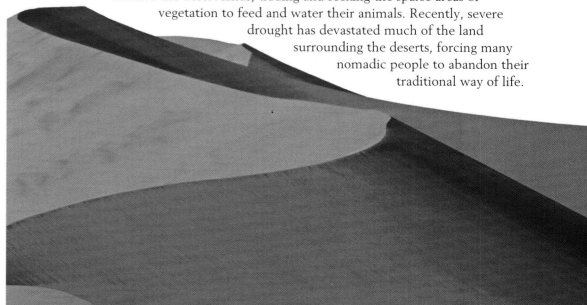

Drought

Many people in Africa suffer greatly because of the hot, dry climate. Countries such as Chad, Burkina Faso and Nigeria can often go for many weeks without rain. The land becomes dusty and infertile, and crops cannot be grown. Thousands of starving families are forced to leave their homes in search of food and aid.

Central and Southern Africa

The mighty River Congo flows from the dense rainforests of Central Africa to the Atlantic Ocean. The terrain in the east of the area is defined by the Great Rift Valley, parts of which have flooded to produce long, deep lakes. Much of Central and Southern Africa has a hot climate with abundant rain, making some regions ideal for farming. Crops such as tea and coffee are grown on large plantations. Most farmers in this area, however, own smaller pieces of land, and can often only produce enough food to feed themselves and their families.

Twenty countries make up Central and Southern Africa. Many were occupied by Europeans during the 1700s and 1800s.

Oil, copper, diamonds and uranium are found in this area, but countries may lack the money to exploit these reserves. South Africa's fertile land, plus its gold, diamonds and uranium, have made the area very wealthy. Successful industries in Central and Southern Africa include textile manufacture in Uganda and the Democratic Republic of Congo, and the mining of manganese in Gabon.

Precious ivory

Many thousands of elephants have been killed by Africans and Europeans for their ivory tusks. Although many countries in Africa and around the world have now banned the ivory trade, illegal poaching is still endangering African elephants.

fact chart

SOMALIA
Area: 637,660 sq km (246,202 sq mi)
Population: 9,500,000
Languages: Somali and Arabic
Currency: Somali shilling

KENYA
Area: 582,650 sq km (224,961 sq mi)
Population: 28,300,000
Languages: Swahili
Currency: Kenya shilling

TANZANIA
Area: 945,040 sq km (364,900 sq mi)
Population: 29,000,000
Languages: Swahili and English
Currency: Tanzanian shilling

UGANDA
Area: 236,860 sq km (91,452 sq mi)
Population: 19,500,000
Languages: English
Currency: Uganda shilling

RWANDA
Area: 26,340 sq km (10,170 sq mi)
Population: 7,000,000
Languages: Kinyarwanda and French
Currency: Rwanda franc

Whale watching

The coast of South Africa is one of the best whale-watching locations in the world. The area is home to the Southern Right Whale, so called because it was once considered the "right" whale to hunt for oil. The species was granted international protection in 1935.

Buried treasure

The city of Witwatersand, in South Africa, is home to the world's largest gold mine. Large tunnels are drilled deep into the ground. Miners are lowered into these tunnels and search for nuggets of gold embedded in the rock and earth.

Early people

Deep within the rocks of the Great Rift Valley, archaeologists have discovered some of the oldest human remains ever found. Fossils of human beings dug up in Kenya have been dated to over two million year ago. Many scientists believe that modern humans originated in East Africa.

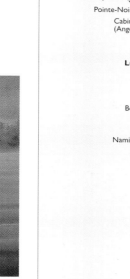

Woolly income

Many different species of cattle, sheep and goats are raised in Southern Africa. Merino sheep in South Africa produce over half of the continent's wool, and angora goats in Lesotho are reared for wool and mohair. Wool products are exported from the area all over the world.

Tourism

Kenya is one of the most popular tourist destinations in Africa. People travel from all over the world to watch the many fascinating species of animals here. Tourism is playing a vital part in the conservation of these species. Many have been hunted illegally for their skins, but money generated by tourism helps the Kenyan government to establish national parks in which the animals are protected.

Sporting heroes

Some of the world's greatest athletes come from high-altitude regions of eastern Africa. The higher the altitude, the less oxygen there is in the air. By training in these conditions, athletes build up large lung capacities, allowing their bodies to perform much more efficiently. When these men and women take part in athletic games around the world, especially at lower altitudes, their increased lung capacities help them to compete at the highest level.

OCEANIA

Australia is almost as large as Europe or the United States of America, so it is not surprising that its landscape is very varied. The central deserts are hot and dry. To the east of the landmass are the mountains and hills of the Great Dividing Range. Between these and the coast there is more fertile ground, with a wetter climate. It is here that most of the population lives.

To the north of Australia is a large island. Its western half belongs to Indonesia. Its eastern half is Papua New Guinea. Here thick forests and a mountainous interior have kept the native people relatively isolated from the outside world.

● Extraordinary mammals

Millions of years ago, Australasia was attached to the other landmasses of the Earth in one huge continent. When it broke away, the plants and animals there, such as this koala, evolved in their own way. Marsupials, such as kangaroos and wombats, which carry their young in a pouch, are found nowhere else in the world.

The many islands that make up the rest of Oceania are divided into groups, some of which may themselves stretch across thousands of miles of ocean. While some are independent, such as Fiji and the Solomon Islands, others are governed by countries as far away as the USA and France.

About 1,600 kilometres (1,000 miles) southeast of Australia is New Zealand, consisting of two main islands. The North Island has a warm climate. The South Island is less populated but has good farm and grazing land.

Map labels

EQUATOR

New Guinea

SOLOMON ISLANDS

PAPUA NEW GUINEA

SOLOMON SEA

ARAFURA SEA

Torres Strait

VANUATU

TIMOR SEA

N
W — E
S

Daly

Roper

CORAL SEA

Great Barrier Reef

FIJI

INDIAN OCEAN

Victoria

Mitchell

KIMBERLEY PLATEAU

Fitzroy

TANAMI DESERT

Flinders

GREAT DIVIDING RANGE

New Caledonia

GREAT SANDY DESERT

Georgina

Fortescue

▲ Mt. Bruce

MACDONNELL RANGES

Diamantina

PACIFIC OCEAN

GIBSON DESERT

▲ Uluru (Ayers Rock)

Simpson Desert

Murchison

AUSTRALIA

Thomson

GREAT VICTORIA DESERT

Darling

GREAT DIVIDING RANGE

NULLARBOR PLAIN

Lachlan

SOUTHERN OCEAN

Murray

GREAT DIVIDING RANGE

Mt. Kosciusko

NEW ZEALAND

Ruapehu

TASMAN SEA

Mt. Cook ▲

SOUTHERN ALPS

Named after the Pacific Ocean, Oceania consists of a few large landmasses and thousands of much smaller islands spread over a huge area. As the largest land mass is Australia, the continent is often called Australasia.

Thousands of islands

The islands of the Pacific stretch across a huge area of ocean. Some are inhabited, but others are only a few metres across. The island below is called an atoll. It is formed when coral grows around a volcanic island. When movements of the Earth's surface make this sink, the coral remains, forming an atoll with a lagoon in the middle.

Great Barrier Reef

Stretching along the northeast coast of Australia, the Great Barrier Reef is made up of over 300 different kinds of coral. It is home to thousands of species of sealife. The coral itself is made of the bodies of tiny polyps that live together in colonies. Damage from humans and from a creature called the crown-of-thorns starfish is endangering the reef, which is now officially protected.

Power from the ground

In the North Island of New Zealand there are hot springs. Sometimes water under pressure is forced out of the ground in geysers up to 70 metres (230 feet) high. The steam from these underwater springs can be used to generate electricity.

Grazing lands

New Zealand has excellent grazing lands for sheep and cattle. In fact, there are over 20 sheep for every one person! New Zealand exports more lamb and dairy produce than any other country.

fact chart

OCEANIA
- Area: 8,508,238 sq km (3,285,048 sq mi)
- Largest lake: Lake Eyre (dry for some months of the year), 9,583 sq km (3,700 sq mi)
- Longest rivers: (Australia) Murray–Darling, 3,750 km (2,330 mi); (New Zealand) Waikato, 425 km (264 mi); (Papua New Guinea) Fly, 1,050 km (650 mi)
- Highest mountain: (Papua New Guinea) Mount Wilhelm, 4,509 m (14,793 ft); (New Zealand) Mount Cook 3,764 m (12,376 ft); (Australia) Mount Kosciusko, 2,228 m (7,310 ft)
- Lowest point: Lake Eyre (Australia), −15 m (−49 ft)
- Largest structure made by living things (in the world): Great Barrier Reef, 2,000 km (1,243 mi) long

The International Date Line passes through the Pacific Ocean. East of this imaginary line the date is a day earlier than it is west of the line. The line passes to the east of New Zealand and Fiji.

The red rock

In the centre of Australia is a huge sandstone outcrop known as Uluru. It is a sacred site for Australia's native people, but is also visited by thousands of tourists every year. It is particularly beautiful at sunset, when it has an astonishingly rich colour.

Australia and New Zealand

Australia is the sixth largest country in the world but has a relatively small population. This is partly because the centre of the country, known as the Outback, consists of thousands of miles of desert and scrubland. Most of Australia's population lives around the coasts, where the climate is temperate.

Australian Aboriginals, the country's first inhabitants, lived nomadic lives, using extraordinary skills to survive in harsh conditions. In 1770, James Cook claimed Australia as British territory. Australia still has strong links with Britain, although immigration from many other parts of the world has enriched its culture. Unfortunately, these developments have often had a negative impact on the way of life of Australia's first people, who continue to fight for better conditions.

Australia's economy is based largely on farming and mining. Modern farming methods mean that crops and livestock can make the most of the vast areas available to them. Huge natural deposits of bauxite (a material used to make aluminum) and iron ore have made Australia a very wealthy country.

New Zealand was one of the last places on Earth to be populated by humans when the Maoris arrived in the tenth century AD. Although sheep and dairy farming are the country's most important sources of income, the timber trade and the electronic industry are vital to the New Zealand economy.

In the beginning

Despite being the original inhabitants of Australia, Aboriginal people now form less than two percent of the population. They fight to preserve their unique customs and heritage in the form of traditional arts and ceremonies. Much of Aboriginal culture revolves around the idea of the Dreamtime, the time when all life was created on Earth.

Flying doctors

Although most of Australia's population lives in built-up areas around the coast, some people choose to settle in remote regions of the Outback, hundreds of miles from the nearest town. Children are taught by the School of the Air Scheme, where lessons are conducted by two-way radio and computer. In a medical emergency, doctors fly out from larger towns and cities.

Water sports

The powerful surf and beautiful beaches of Australia have helped make the country famous for its water sports. People travel from all over the world to water-ski, surf and sail in Australia's warm waters. Bondi Beach, in southeast Australia, is famous for its surfing waters, and many tournaments are held here each year.

Eco-energy

Over thirty huge dams can be found in New Zealand, blocking fast-flowing rivers. The water passes through controlled channels in the dam, powering generators that produce electricity. Over eighty percent of the country's electricity is produced by environmentally friendly hydroelectric plants, helping to make New Zealand one of the cleanest countries in the world.

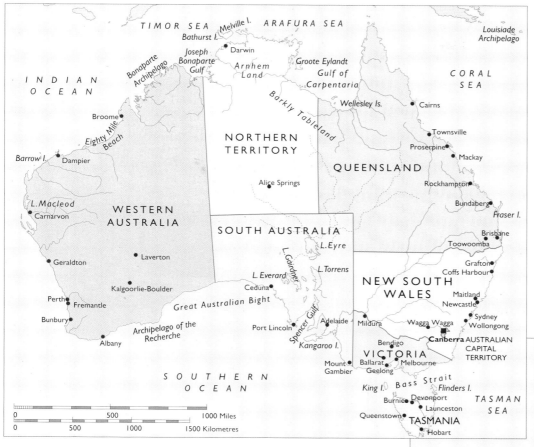

fact chart

AUSTRALIA
- Area: 7,682,300 sq km (2,966,136 sq mi)
- Population: 18,700,000
- Languages: English
- Currency: Australian dollar

NEW ZEALAND
- Area: 268,860 sq km (103,807 sq mi)
- Population: 3,800,000
- Languages: English
- Currency: New Zealand dollar

PAPUA NEW GUINEA
- Area: 462,840 sq km (178,703 sq mi)
- Population: 4,000,000
- Languages: English
- Currency: Kina

● Sydney

Although not the capital of Australia, Sydney is by far its largest and busiest city. It is built around a harbour, with the north and south of the city linked by the famous Sydney Bridge, built in 1932. The most elaborate of Sydney's buildings is the Opera House, which has sail-like segments rising above the water.

● Forest fires

Parts of Australia are covered by vast forests known as the bush. In the intense heat of summer, the bush becomes very dry, and there is often a serious threat of fire. A carelessly discarded cigarette or a spark from a campfire is enough to start a blaze that can spread for hundreds of miles. These bushfires devastate everything in their paths, including houses, wildlife and farms.

THE POLES

The bitterly cold region of the Arctic consists of everything that lies north of the Arctic Circle. This includes parts of Europe, Asia and America, and the largest island in the world, Greenland. These lands surround the Arctic Ocean, which is frozen for most of the year. The mainland areas of the Arctic are mostly made up of tundra. Reindeer, arctic foxes and caribou can be found in the summer grazing on the sparse vegetation, and seals, walruses and whales populate the Arctic Ocean.

The Antarctic is the world's fifth largest continent, surrounded by the Southern Ocean. The conditions here are so hostile that it is the only place on Earth with no permanent human population.

The Arctic has vast reserves of oil, natural gas and minerals. Antarctica is also rich in minerals. In 1991, 12 of the world's most powerful nations agreed that mining in Antarctica would be banned for 50 years to preserve this unique habitat.

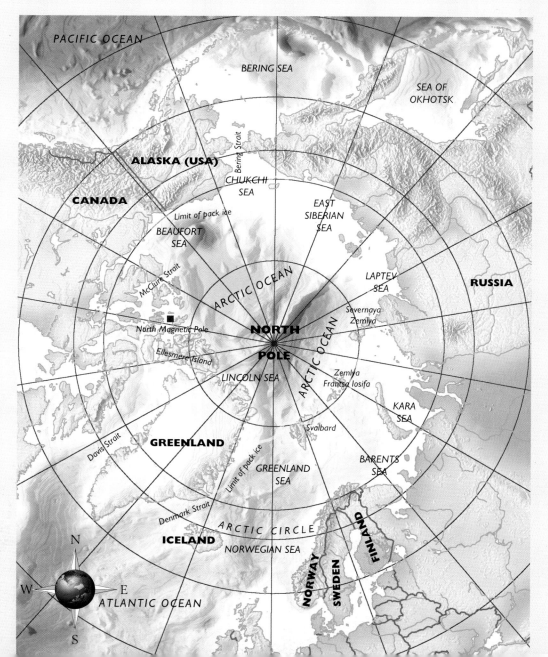

● Ice-breakers

Early European explorers sailed to the Arctic region in search of the Northwest Passage, a trade route around North America to Asia. The giant sheets of ice that covered the oceans often hampered their progress or even trapped their ships for months on end. The ships that travel across the Arctic Ocean today are called ice-breakers because they have very powerful engines and strong bows to cut through the ice.

● People of the Arctic

Despite the climate, many different peoples live in the Arctic region. The Inuit of northern Canada traditionally survived by hunting fish, whales and reindeer. Such ways of life are ending.

fact chart

ARCTIC
● Area: 9,500,000 sq km (3,668,000 sq mi)

ANTARCTICA
● Area: 14,000,000 sq km (5,405,400 sq mi)

At the far north and far south of the Earth lie two regions of ice and snow, the Arctic and the Antarctic.

Scientists in the Antarctic

Most visitors to the Antarctic are scientists. Some study damage to the ozone layer—a layer of gases in the Earth's atmosphere that protects the planet from harmful radiation.

Midnight Sun

Because the Sun rotates at a slight angle, during the long winter months in the Arctic it never rises above the horizon. It is dark all day, and temperatures may drop lower than –70°C (–94°F). At midsummer, the Sun never sets.

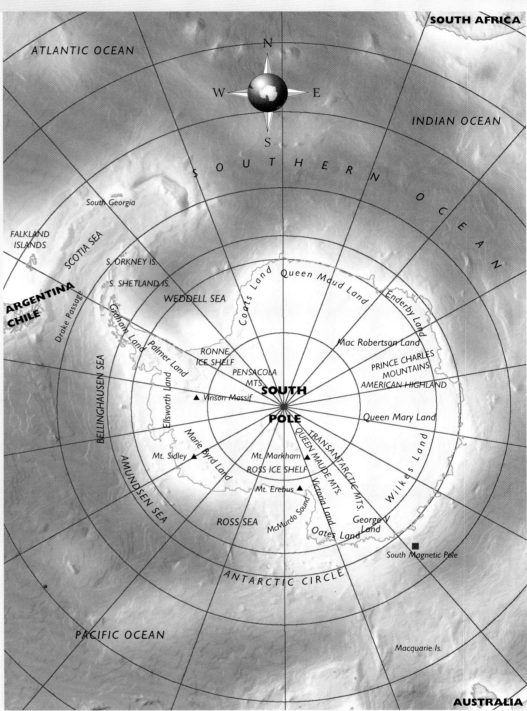

SOUTH AFRICA

ATLANTIC OCEAN

INDIAN OCEAN

SOUTHERN OCEAN

South Georgia

FALKLAND ISLANDS

SCOTIA SEA

S. ORKNEY IS.

S. SHETLAND IS.

ARGENTINA CHILE

Drake Passage

WEDDELL SEA

Coats Land

Queen Maud Land

Enderby Land

Mac Robertson Land

PRINCE CHARLES MOUNTAINS

AMERICAN HIGHLAND

Graham Land

Palmer Land

RONNE ICE SHELF

PENSACOLA MTS.

BELLINGHAUSEN SEA

Ellsworth Land

▲ Vinson Massif

SOUTH POLE

Queen Mary Land

Marie Byrd Land

Mt. Sidley ▲

Mt. Markham ▲

ROSS ICE SHELF

QUEEN MAUDE MTS.

TRANSANTARCTIC MTS.

Wilkes Land

AMUNDSEN SEA

Mt. Erebus ▲

Victoria Land

ROSS SEA

McMurdo Sound

Oates Land

George V Land

■ South Magnetic Pole

ANTARCTIC CIRCLE

PACIFIC OCEAN

Macquarie Is.

AUSTRALIA

Wildlife of the cold

Most parts of the Arctic are populated by polar bears, which prey on seals that come up from below the ice to breathe. Bears can pose a threat to human communities in the Arctic region, and some towns now even have "polar bear jails" where the animals are kept until they can be safely airlifted away from the inhabited area.

Polar lights

The beautiful light-show called the Aurora Borealis in the Arctic and the Aurora Australis in the Antarctic is caused by charged particles from the Sun interacting with gases in the Earth's atmosphere.

Fact Section

ANTIGUA & BARBUDA
- Area: 440 sq km (169 sq mi)
- Population: 67,000
- Languages: English
- Currency: East Caribbean dollar

BAHAMAS
- Area: 13,860 sq km (5,353 sq mi)
- Population: 300,000
- Languages: English
- Currency: Bahamian dollar

BARBADOS
- Area: 430 sq km (166 sq mi)
- Population: 300,000
- Languages: English
- Currency: Barbados dollar

DOMINICA
- Area: 750 sq km (290 sq mi)
- Population: 72,000
- Languages: English
- Currency: East Caribbean dollar

DOMINICAN REPUBLIC
- Area: 48,730 sq km (18,815 sq mi)
- Population: 7,600,000
- Languages: Spanish
- Currency: Peso

FALKLAND ISLANDS
- Area: 1,815 sq km (700 sq mi)
- Population: 2,000
- Languages: English
- Currency: Falkland Island pound

FRENCH GUIANA
- Area: 90,000 sq km (34,750 sq mi)
- Population: 114,800
- Languages: French
- Currency: French franc

GRENADA
- Area: 345 sq km (131 sq mi)
- Population: 92,000
- Languages: English
- Currency: East Caribbean dollar

GUYANA
- Area: 214,970 sq km (83,000 sq mi)
- Population: 820,000
- Languages: English
- Currency: Guyana dollar

HAITI
- Area: 27,750 sq km (10,714 sq mi)
- Population: 6,900,000
- Languages: French, Creole
- Currency: Gourde

JAMAICA
- Area: 10,990 sq km (4,244 sq mi)
- Population: 2,400,000
- Languages: English
- Currency: Jamaican dollar

MEXICO
- Area: 1,967,190 sq km (761,604 sq mi)
- Population: 92,000,000
- Languages: Spanish
- Currency: Mexican new peso

THE PHILIPPINES
- Area: 300,000 sq km (115,830 sq mi)
- Population: 65,700,000
- Languages: Pilipino and English
- Currency: Philippino peso

PUERTO RICO
- Area: 8,959 sq km (3,459 sq mi)
- Population: 3,650,000
- Languages: Spanish
- Currency: US dollar

ST KITTS AND NEVIS
- Area: 360 sq km (140 sq mi)
- Population: 42,000
- Languages: English
- Currency: East Caribbean dollar

ST LUCIA
- Area: 620 sq km (239 sq mi)
- Population: 139,000
- Languages: English
- Currency: East Caribbean dollar

ST VINCENT AND THE GRENADINES
- Area: 340 sq km (131 sq mi)
- Population: 111,000
- Languages: English
- Currency: East Caribbean dollar

SURINAM
- Area: 163,820 sq km (63,040 sq mi)
- Population: 450,000
- Languages: Dutch
- Currency: Surinam guilder

TRINIDAD AND TOBAGO
- Area: 5,130 sq km (1,980 sq mi)
- Population: 1,300,000
- Languages: English
- Currency: Trinidad and Tobago dollar

TURKS AND CAICOS
- Area: 430 sq km (166 sq mi)
- Population: 13,000
- Languages: English
- Currency: US dollar

BAHRAIN
- Area: 680 sq km (263 sq mi)
- Population: 600,000
- Languages: Arabic
- Currency: Bahrain dinar

BANGLADESH
- Area: 143,998 sq km (55,598 sq mi)
- Population: 121,671,000
- Languages: Bengali
- Currency: Taka

BHUTAN
- Area: 47,000 sq km (18,147 sq mi)
- Population: 1,650,000
- Languages: Dzonghka
- Currency: Ngultrum

BRUNEI
- Area: 5,770 sq km (2,228 sq mi)
- Population: 276,000
- Languages: Malay
- Currency: Brunei dollar

CAMBODIA
- Area: 181,040 sq km (69,900 sq mi)
- Population: 9,300,000
- Languages: Khmer
- Currency: Riel

CYPRUS
- Area: 9,250 sq km (3,572 sq mi)
- Population: 720,000
- Languages: Greek and Turkish
- Currency: Cyprus pound and Turkish lira

KUWAIT
- Area: 17,820 sq km (6,880 sq mi)
- Population: 2,000,000
- Languages: Arabic
- Currency: Kuwaiti dinar

KYRGYZSTAN
- Area: 198,500 sq km (76,641 sq mi)
- Population: 4,500,000
- Languages: Kyrgyz
- Currency: Som

LAOS
- Area: 236,800 sq km (91,429 sq mi)
- Population: 4,600,000
- Languages: Lao
- Currency: Kip

LEBANON
- Area: 10,400 sq km (4,015 sq mi)
- Population: 2,901,000
- Languages: Arabic
- Currency: Lebanese pound

MYANMAR
- Area: 676,580 sq km (261,217 sq mi)
- Population: 44,700,000
- Languages: Burmese
- Currency: Kyat

NORTH KOREA
- Area: 120,548 sq km (46,541 sq mi)
- Population: 23,100,000
- Languages: Korean
- Currency: Won

OMAN
- Area: 300,000 sq km (105,020 sq mi)
- Population: 1,650,000
- Languages: Arabic
- Currency: Omani rial

QATAR
- Area: 11,000 sq km (4,247 sq mi)
- Population: 550,000
- Languages: Arabic
- Currency: Qatar riyal

SOUTH KOREA
- Area: 99,020 sq km (38,232 sq mi)
- Population: 43,419,900
- Languages: Korean
- Currency: Won

TAJIKISTAN
- Area: 143,100 sq km (55,251 sq mi)
- Population: 5,200,000
- Languages: Tajik
- Currency: Rouble

THAILAND
- Area: 513,120 sq km (198,117 sq mi)
- Population: 56,900,000
- Languages: Thai
- Currency: Baht

TURKMENISTAN
- Area: 488,100 sq km (188,456 sq mi)
- Population: 3,500,000
- Languages: Turkmen
- Currency: Manat

UNITED ARAB EMIRATES
- Area: 83,600 sq km (32,278 sq mi)
- Population: 1,750,000
- Languages: Arabic
- Currency: UAE dirham

YEMEN
- Area: 531,000 sq km (205,019 sq mi)
- Population: 12,500,000
- Languages: Arabic
- Currency: Yemen riyal

ANGOLA
- Area: 1,246,700 sq km (481,353 sq mi)
- Population: 10,300,000
- Languages: Portuguese
- Currency: Kwanza

BENIN
- Area: 112,620 sq km (43,483 sq mi)
- Population: 5,100,000
- Languages: French
- Currency: Franc CFA

BOTSWANA
- Area: 581,730 sq km (224,607 sq mi)
- Population: 1,350,000
- Languages: English
- Currency: Pula

BURKINA FASO
- Area: 274,400 sq km (105,945 sq mi)
- Population: 10,000,000
- Languages: French
- Currency: Franc CFA

BURUNDI
- Area: 27,830 sq km (10,745 sq mi)
- Population: 5,900,000
- Languages: Kirundi and French
- Currency: Burundi franc

CAMEROON
- Area: 475,440 sq km (183,568 sq mi)
- Population: 12,500,000
- Languages: French and English
- Currency: Franc CFA

CAPE VERDE ISLANDS
- Area: 4,030 sq km (1,556 sq mi)
- Population: 400,000
- Languages: Portuguese
- Currency: Cape Verde escudo

CENTRAL AFRICAN REPUBLIC
- Area: 624,975 sq km (241,302 sq mi)
- Population: 3,300,000
- Languages: French
- Currency: Franc CFA

CHAD
- Area: 1,284,000 sq km (495,755 sq mi)
- Population: 6,100,000
- Languages: Arabic and French
- Currency: franc CFA

CONGO
- Area: 342,000 sq km (132,047 sq mi)
- Population: 2,500,000
- Languages: French
- Currency: Franc CFA

CÔTE D'IVOIRE (IVORY COAST)
- Area: 322,460 sq km (124,504 sq mi)
- Population: 13,500,000
- Languages: French
- Currency: Franc CFA

DEMOCRATIC REPUBLIC OF CONGO
- Area: 2,344,880 sq km (905,358 sq mi)
- Population: 42,000,000
- Languages: French
- Currency: Congo franc

DJIBOUTI
- Area: 23,200 sq km (8,958 sq mi)
- Population: 500,000
- Languages: Arabic and French
- Currency: Djibouti franc

EQUATORIAL GUINEA
- Area: 28,050 sq km (10,830 sq mi)
- Population: 380,000
- Languages: Spanish
- Currency: Franc CFA

ERITREA
- Area: 93,680 sq km (36,170 sq mi)
- Population: 3,500,000
- Languages: Tigrinya and Arabic
- Currency: Ethiopian birr

GABON
- Area: 267,670 sq km (103,348 sq mi)
- Population: 1,050,000
- Languages: French
- Currency: Franc CFA

GAMBIA
- Area: 11,290 sq km (4,363 sq mi)
- Population: 900,000
- Languages: English
- Currency: Dalasi

GHANA
- Area: 238,537 sq km (92,101 sq mi)
- Population: 16,400,000
- Languages: English
- Currency: Cedi

GUINEA
- Area: 245,860 sq km (94,926 sq mi)
- Population: 5,600,000
- Languages: French
- Currency: Guinean franc

GUINEA-BISSAU
- Area: 36,120 sq km (13,946 sq mi)
- Population: 1,050,000
- Languages: Portuguese
- Currency: Guinea-Bissau peso

LESOTHO
- Area: 30,350 sq km (11,718 sq mi)
- Population: 1,880,000
- Languages: Sesotho and English
- Currency: Loti

LIBERIA
- Area: 111,370 sq km (43,000 sq mi)
- Population: 2,820,000
- Languages: English
- Currency: Liberian dollar

MADAGASCAR
- Area: 587,040 sq km (226,657 sq mi)
- Population: 13,300,000
- Languages: Malagasy and French
- Currency: Malagasy franc

MALAWI
- Area: 118,840 sq km (45,884 sq mi)
- Population: 9,200,000
- Languages: Chichewa and English
- Currency: Kwacha

MALI
- Area: 1,240,190 sq km (478,840 sq mi)
- Population: 10,140,000
- Languages: French
- Currency: Franc CFA

MAURITANIA
- Area: 1,030,700 sq km (397,953 sq mi)
- Population: 2,210,000
- Languages: Arabic and French
- Currency: Ouguiya

MOZAMBIQUE
- Area: 799,380 sq km (309,405 sq mi)
- Population: 15,400,000
- Languages: Portuguese
- Currency: Metical

NAMIBIA
- Area: 824,270 sq km (318,258 sq mi)
- Population: 1,600,000
- Languages: English
- Currency: Namibian dollar

NIGER
- Area: 1,267,000 sq km (48,919 sq mi)
- Population: 8,400,000
- Languages: French
- Currency: Franc CFA

SAO TOMÉ AND PRINCIPE
- Area: 1,000 sq km (386 sq mi)
- Population: 122,000
- Languages: Portuguese
- Currency: Dobra

SENEGAL
- Area: 197,160 sq km (76,123 sq mi)
- Population: 8,800,000
- Languages: French
- Currency: Franc CFA

SOUTH AFRICA
- Area: 1,127,000 sq km (435,134 sq mi)
- Population: 40,800,000
- Languages: English, Afrikaans and many local African languages
- Currency: Rand

SUDAN
- Area: 2,505,810 sq km (967,498 sq mi)
- Population: 28,000,000
- Languages: Arabic
- Currency: Sudanese dinar

SWAZILAND
- Area: 17,360 sq km (6,703 sq mi)
- Population: 814,000
- Languages: English and Swazi
- Currency: Lilangeni

TOGO
- Area: 56,780 sq km (21,927 sq mi)
- Population: 3,900,000
- Languages: French, Kabye and Ewe
- Currency: Franc CFA

TUNISIA
- Area: 163,610 sq km (63,170 sq mi)
- Population: 8,610,000
- Languages: Arabic
- Currency: Tunisian dinar

WESTERN SAHARA
- Area: 252,120 sq km (97,344 sq mi)
- Population: 261,000
- Languages: Arabic
- Currency: Dirham

ZAMBIA
- Area: 752,610 sq km (290,584 sq mi)
- Population: 8,900,000
- Languages: English
- Currency: Kwacha

ZIMBABWE
- Area: 390,580 sq km (150,804 sq mi)
- Population: 10,410,000
- Languages: English
- Currency: Zimbabwe dollar

Gazetteer